The International
Marine

LOG

BOOK

A complete log-keeping system

C. DALE NOUSE

The Log of

_____

First Entry

_____

Last Entry

_____

14 15 16 17 18 19 20   LCR   23 22 21
ISBN 978-0-07-048237-1
MHID 0-07-048237-3

*Library of Congress Cataloging-in-Publication Data is available
from the Library of Congress.*

This publication is designed to provide accurate and authoritative information in regard to the subject matter covered. It is sold with the understanding that neither the author nor the publisher is engaged in rendering legal, accounting, securities trading, or other professional services. If legal advice or other expert assistance is required, the services of a competent professional person should be sought.
From a Declaration of Principles Jointly Adopted by a Committee of the American Bar Association and a Committee of Publishers and Association

International Marine/McGraw-Hill books are available at special quantity discounts to use as premiums and sales promotions or for use in boating or sailing programs. To contact a representative, please e-mail us at bulksales@mcgraw-hill.com. This book is printed on acid-free paper.

Questions regarding the content of this book should be addressed to
www.internationalmarine.com

Questions regarding the ordering of this book should be addressed to
The McGraw-Hill Companies
Customer Service Department
P.O. Box 547
Blacklick, OH 43004
Retail customers: 1-800-262-4729
Bookstores: 1-800-722-4726

This book was typeset in Adobe Garamond and Helvetica.

Contents

Passages

Date	Origin and Destination	Page

Date	Origin and Destination	Page

Foreword

IN VERY OLDEN TIMES, a ship's hour-by-hour progress on a passage was recorded on an often beautifully carved "traverse board," a keyhole-shaped device with concentric rings on a compass rose. With each bell of a watch, a peg from a bundle attached to the board with leather thongs was inserted in a hole to indicate the ship's course. A separate grid below was used to "peg" the ship's speed. Woe to the watch officer who failed to keep speed and heading on this important "cribbage board."

In less antiquarian times, the same function was served by the "rough log," a collection of notations from which was devised at noon each day the "smooth log" or "abstract log," the cleaned-up version presented to the land-based owner of the ship.

Nowadays, they're called "yacht logs" and, too often, they are complicated, pretentious gift items that won't lie flat, serve too many purposes (or not enough), demand the services of a Dickensian Bob Cratchit, and fall apart at the first slight wetting.

Aboard *Coup Fourré*, my 32-foot ketch, we call ours the "on-deck log," so named in a casual moment by my Number-One son, Todd Westen Nouse, because on deck is where it belongs.

Developed and refined endlessly over three decades of groping about the water, the on-deck log serves essential needs, yet can be used to record a great deal of information. It is flexible, to match your inclination to transcribe anything from bare piloting details to names and anecdotes that are valuable or enjoyable to recall.

Here's what the log can do for you, with some actual examples taken from *Coup Fourré's* on-deck log.

• Most importantly, a log encourages good piloting by training you to keep exact track of where you are and where you're going—and to avoid the places where it's not at all good to be.

While singlehanding north along the western shore of Ontario's Bruce Peninsula in Lake Huron several years ago,

I simply could not find a little buoy marking a nasty shelf a mile or so off Clark Point. I was forced to slow down and swing a mile or so wide of the point to be safe. Several weeks later, when returning singlehanded from the North Channel, my son Todd read the log for my Kincardine-Goderich leg, looked extra hard for the buoy, found it and was greatly relieved to not have to waste 15 or 20 minutes.

• The log trains you to be a careful weather observer, to note changes in weather conditions—and may help you avoid being blind-sided by a rolling, black squall line.

Moving *Coup Fourré* one warm spring day from the boatyard to my mooring, a distance of but a dozen miles, I logged the 7 a.m. weather forecast, which was fine. However, because the inevitable odd jobs delayed my departure, I didn't get under way until shortly before noon. For failing to recheck the forecast, I was treated to a half-hour's torment by one of those fierce spring squalls that pop out of nowhere.

• Although this is a logbook for your own boat, it can be used to record your sailing vacations aboard friends' boats or aboard charter boats. If you charter frequently, you even could have a separate log for charter trips.

Aboard a Seastream 43 chartered in Scotland, we decided after lingering over lunch at a fine little bay, to slip up a tight channel between the Isle of Skye and the mainland to another harbor. We had noted in the log on the first day of the charter that the big motorsailer would do 8 knots with her Mercedes diesel working hard. However, a check of the pilot data clearly indicated an adverse tidal current in the channel of 6 knots. A simple calculation plainly indicated there was not enough daylight. Because only the foolhardy tempt the waters around the Isle of Skye after dark, we stayed put.

• The log book stimulates you to never leave without first

running through a quick, simple but vital checklist similar to that routinely used by prudent airplane pilots.

Before leaving Newport, Rhode Island, for a weekend trip to Cuttyhunk, *Coup Fourré* had her mid-season engine oil and filter change. Early the next morning, before getting under way, the oil again was checked. A heavy oil slick floated on top of the inevitable bilge water. In changing the filter, the seal had not seated properly. It took but a few minutes to correct. Because it was a windless morning, failure to again check the oil could have proved costly and perhaps spoiled the weekend.

• Although not designed to serve as a legal document, the on-deck log will have some legal status in the event of trouble, especially if you make careful and methodical log entries.

In the U.S., the only log specified by law is the "Official Log Book," which is required only for ships of 75 gross tons or more and engaged in foreign trade. Issued and overseen by the Coast Guard, this very traditional log is primarily a ship's personnel record. In it are recorded all crew information, deaths and serious illnesses, crimes aboard and punishment meted out. It even has in the back a "Slop and Cash Account," in which is recorded crew's personal supplies and cash loans. This developed from the time-honored "Slops" or "Slop Chest," from which crewmen bought (for cash or credit) clothes, rigging knives and other personal supplies. The Coast Guard's "Official Log Book" also must display the ship's draft on entering and leaving harbors; fire and boat drills; damage to the ship or crew casualties, refueling, etc. The log generally is kept by a ship's purser, which gave rise to the old seaman's expression "purser's grin," which means a sardonic smile. Besides the "Official Log Book," meticulously operated big ships have many other logs—engine logs, deck logs (which may include weather notations), radar bearing logs (often the basic navigation log), radio logs and AMVER (Automated Merchant Vessel Emergency Rescue) logs. Some in-harbor tugs use a common, bound diary to record their activities. All such logs, of which there are many commercial varieties, have numbered pages and are sewn-bound to preclude whole page substitutions. If you wish to make this log more acceptable legally, have a notary consecutively number each page by hand in permanent ink and affix a seal on the first or last numbered page. Even without such numbering, and even if written in pencil (as we do aboard *Coup Fourré*), this log will have considerable legal standing, especially if you are an accurate and consistent log keeper.

• The on-deck log can be a fine record of special harbor information, such as useful names and telephone numbers.

Some friends from Grosse Pointe, Michigan, pulled into Port Elgin, Ontario, on Lake Huron with an engine malfunction on their Seawind ketch. Because we'd had a water-temperature gauge problem there several years earlier, a quick check of our log turned up the name and home telephone of the town's best and most accommodating marine mechanic. Although the mechanic had since changed jobs, he came down at dinner time and, with some quick adjustments, quickly solved the problem.

• The log can be a compendium of interesting information about your boat.

My son once saw in a harbor a Mariner 32 like ours that had been dismasted, the wood mainmast splintered about 10 feet above the deck. Todd noted the boat's name and home yacht club in the log. That winter, with a couple of telephone calls, I located the owner and learned that he believed he had lost the mast because his crew had inadvertently tightened the upper shrouds and left the lowers slack—the reverse of the proper practice for tuning ketch rigs.

If you've never experienced the tension of dropping oil pressure or dying batteries; been sorely vexed by a holding tank oozing unmentionable fluid along the lee deck; had to explain to guests why there is no more fresh water, or got your knickers in a twist when the fog closed in after you forgot to make a note of the last two buoys, you probably don't need to keep a log.

However, for truly safe and pleasurable cruising, we who've sailed aboard *Coup Fourré* strongly suggest you acquire the habit.

C. Dale Nouse, Executive Editor
Practical Sailor magazine
Newport, Rhode Island
Spring, 1997

How Best to Use Your Log

THE FIRST PAIR OF PAGES of your new log are an actual day in the cruising life of the ketch *Coup Fourré*. Remove the pages if you like. They are included only by way of explaining the on-deck log. The sample should be largely self-explanatory. However, a few tips might be in order.

- A pair of facing pages comprises one day—with the option of running over to another pair of pages if the pilotage entries so require or if you're on a two-day or longer passage.
- In the upper left corner—the "Morning Checklist"— we require on *Coup Fourré* a comment and an initial for each item. If something is not checked, such as "Transmission," it is intentionally noted as "not checked." Fuel, water, and holding tanks rarely have gauges, but the checklist requires that they be given thought or checked against when last filled or pumped out. Seacocks should be deliberately opened or closed. In any event they should be operated frequently to assure they are not frozen. Three spaces are left for electronic equipment; radio checks should be mandatory.
- At the top right are weather abbreviations, easy to note and record. If you wish, you can mark the first weather forecast with a circle around each predicted condition. The second set of forecast conditions can be checked, the third underlined, etc., with the time of each forecast listed under "Notes." Or, if you wish, you can write the forecast under "Notes" and use the listed data to display actual observed conditions at various times.
- On the top page, under the "Notes" column, we usually record the time in civil time because these entries often are shore-based activities. If you prefer, you can use either civil time or the 2400 system. The latter has the advantage of being slightly easier to use in arithmetic calculations—which is why we record pilotage times in the 2400 system.

- On the bottom half of the pair of pages, under the time column, we enter major or important times in the first column and less important times in the column set off with a dotted line. In an earlier version of *Coup Fourré*'s log, we had but one time column, but that arrangement led to some confusion and some errors in calculating distance run and estimated times of arrival (ETAs). So, the second column was added and the first column was reserved for major waypoints.
- Under the "Course" column, you can use compass—magnetic or true, as you wish. We use compass heading and do whatever calculations may be necessary on a shorthand notebook that usually is kicking around the cockpit or the chart table. Using the compass course in the log makes it easier for the helmsman.
- The "Speed" column, displaying either actual readings from a speedometer or estimates, is important for checking the log against waypoints and for working out speed-time-distance problems along the way. It also helps in verifying estimates of currents you may be working with or against.
- The "Miles" column permits easy calculations of distance traveled along the course, based on the odometer (and I hope you have an accurate instrument), with sightings and fixes shown either under the "Pilotage" column or under the "Notes" column.
- We use the "Comments from the Helm" column for most anything, although it's perhaps best to enter chit-chat in the "Notes" column on the top page.
- We use a "tiger clip" on the used-up pages to make the log easy to open to the current day's pages.

  Rather than at noon, which is when old-time ship captains did the day's formal logbook work, we take a few minutes in the evening (usually when working up chart data and plans for the next day) to total up the "day's work," figure out average speeds, and check over the log entries. Anchoring information, especially if we're in a new or questionable harbor, often is entered in the log, with the anchor or anchors used, the rode, and what we found on the bottom while taking the anchor's-down-let's-go-

swimming break. I keep a good facemask aboard specifically for checking the set of the anchor.

In the morning, whether it's a hustle and bustle effort to get going early or a leisurely departure, it starts all over again with the upper left hand corner of the top page.

Happy cruising!

Morning Checklist		
Check	Comment	Initial
Engine Oil	Almost max.	TWN
Coolant	Full	TWN
Battery Water	Both up	TWN
Battery Condition #1	10½	TWN
Battery Condition #2	12+	TWN
Transmission	Not checked	(N)
Engine Hours	291.1	(N)
Fuel	Filled, Little Sub	H
Water Tank	" " "	H
Holding Tank	Pumped " "	H
Pumps/Bilge	Both Ok / clear	TWN
Seacocks	All open and free	TWN
Radio and Electronics	VHF Rec. & Send	(N)
Radio and Electronics	RDF O.K.	(N)

Crew and Guests

Dale Nouse
Herb Lueders
Betty Lueders
Todd Nouse

Wind Force	Wind Direction	Sea State	Barometer	Forecast
0-5	N	Glassy	31.00	Fair
6-10 — 6 a.m. TWN	NE	Small Chop	30.75	Rising Wind
11-15 Same.	E	Moderate Chop	30.50	Veering Wind
16-20 Noon	SE	Heavy Chop	30.25	Backing Wind
21-25	S	Ground Swell	30.00	Squalls/Thunderstorms
26-30	SW —	Crossing Seas	29.75	Rain
31-35	W	Boarding Seas	29.50	Fog
35-40	NW	Tide Rips	29.25	Storm
____ other	Variable		29.00	Haze

Time	Notes
7 am.	Forecast: Good day! Clear, 11-16 SW. (N)
7:20	Tea made. Sleeping bags aired. Dale says boat is right! B
9 a.m.	Great breakfast -- oatmeal, rolls, coffee. Dad says E.T.A. Killarney 4 p.m. TWN
Noon	Weather check. No change. See above. H
2 PM.	Big lunch, thanks to Hungry Herb.
5 P.M.	Beautiful spot. We were greeted by Dockmaster Mickey. Skipper says dinner at 8 ashore! Betty
5:30 pm	Got ice from icehouse — 35 lbs — ¼ mi. down road. TWN
5:45 pm	Contacted mechanic rec. by Mickey. Coming at 7 a.m. is: Angus McKeon phone 4509
6 PM	Contacted on VHF, Windswept (Boddys). They're in Little Current. Will meet tomorrow in The Pool. H
11:45 p.m	Little squall went through. Quite a current in channel. Dad and I set extra spring. TWN -- checked weather via radio. Nothing severe. A.M. fine for Bay Finn. Back to bed.

Time	Pilotage	Course	Speed	Log	Miles	Comments from the Helm
0745	Left Big Tub for Kilarney via Wall I.	Visual	5			Ⓝ Very light breeze. 1200 rpm
	0750 Lighthouse Pt. coming to new course	003	6	810.8		Main up. 1,000 rpm
0830	Skinned Echo I. by ½ mi.	003	6	814.5		Betty says she'll serve nice
						breakfast if we sign but
						don't strike White Shingle. TWN
1115	N. tip Wall I. abeam. changed course to	028	6-	828.8	18.0	Engine off. Jib set. Kenyon is
						dead on. Ⓝ
	Noon Rabbit I. abeam to port	030	6.5	839.8		Ft. Straight as an arrow.
	0115 Clay cliff abeam to port, mile off	028	6	839.8		Betty
1210	Campbell Rock buoy. Changed to	014	5.5	845.5	34.7	Found buoy w/ binocs. TWN
1330	S. tip Geo I. abeam, port	014	5.0	853.1		3' following sea Ⓝ
						Geo I. low-lying green
1345	Approaching Jackman Rock, in sight					Sails down. Engine on.
						Enter channel Ⓝ
1615	Docked at Sportsman's Lodge			855.9	45.1	
8h. 30m						
	Day's Work: 45.1					Note: Engine running little hot — 180° Ⓝ
	Avg. Speed: 5.42					
	Avg. Port-to-Port 5.42					

Date: 7/30/96
Day: Tuesday
From: Tobermory
To: Killarney

Page 189

Morning Checklist

Check		Comment	Initial
Engine Oil			
Coolant			
Battery Water			
Battery Condition	#1		
	#2		
Transmission			
Engine Hours			
Fuel			
Water Tank			
Holding Tank			
Pumps/Bilge			
Seacocks			
Radio and Electronics			

Crew and Guests

Wind Force	Wind Direction	Sea State	Barometer	Forecast
0-5	N	Glassy	31.00	Fair
6-10	NE	Small Chop	30.75	Rising Wind
11-15	E	Moderate Chop	30.50	Veering Wind
16-20	SE	Heavy Chop	30.25	Backing Wind
21-25	S	Ground Swell	30.00	Squalls/Thunderstorms
26-30	SW	Crossing Seas	29.75	Rain
31-35	W	Boarding Seas	29.50	Fog
35-40	NW	Tide Rips	29.25	Storm
_____other	Variable		29.00	Haze

Time	Notes

Time		Pilotage	Course	Speed	Log	Miles	Comments from the Helm		
								Day:	Date:
								To:	From:
								Page	

Morning Checklist

Check		Comment	Initial
Engine Oil			
Coolant			
Battery Water			
Battery Condition	#1		
	#2		
Transmission			
Engine Hours			
Fuel			
Water Tank			
Holding Tank			
Pumps/Bilge			
Seacocks			
Radio and Electronics			

Crew and Guests

Wind Force	Wind Direction	Sea State	Barometer	Forecast
0-5	N	Glassy	31.00	Fair
6-10	NE	Small Chop	30.75	Rising Wind
11-15	E	Moderate Chop	30.50	Veering Wind
16-20	SE	Heavy Chop	30.25	Backing Wind
21-25	S	Ground Swell	30.00	Squalls/Thunderstorms
26-30	SW	Crossing Seas	29.75	Rain
31-35	W	Boarding Seas	29.50	Fog
35-40	NW	Tide Rips	29.25	Storm
____other	Variable		29.00	Haze

Time	Notes

Time			Pilotage	Course	Speed	Log	Miles	Comments from the Helm
									Date:
									Day:
									From:
									To:
									Page

Morning Checklist

Check		Comment	Initial
Engine Oil			
Coolant			
Battery Water			
Battery Condition	#1		
	#2		
Transmission			
Engine Hours			
Fuel			
Water Tank			
Holding Tank			
Pumps/Bilge			
Seacocks			
Radio and Electronics			

Crew and Guests

Wind Force	Wind Direction	Sea State	Barometer	Forecast
0-5	N	Glassy	31.00	Fair
6-10	NE	Small Chop	30.75	Rising Wind
11-15	E	Moderate Chop	30.50	Veering Wind
16-20	SE	Heavy Chop	30.25	Backing Wind
21-25	S	Ground Swell	30.00	Squalls/Thunderstorms
26-30	SW	Crossing Seas	29.75	Rain
31-35	W	Boarding Seas	29.50	Fog
35-40	NW	Tide Rips	29.25	Storm
_____other	Variable		29.00	Haze

Time	Notes

Time		Pilotage	Course	Speed	Log	Miles	Comments from the Helm
							Date:
							Day:
							From:
							To:
							Page

Morning Checklist		
Check	Comment	Initial
Engine Oil		
Coolant		
Battery Water		
Battery Condition #1		
Battery Condition #2		
Transmission		
Engine Hours		
Fuel		
Water Tank		
Holding Tank		
Pumps/Bilge		
Seacocks		
Radio and Electronics		

Crew and Guests

Wind Force	Wind Direction	Sea State	Barometer	Forecast
0-5	N	Glassy	31.00	Fair
6-10	NE	Small Chop	30.75	Rising Wind
11-15	E	Moderate Chop	30.50	Veering Wind
16-20	SE	Heavy Chop	30.25	Backing Wind
21-25	S	Ground Swell	30.00	Squalls/Thunderstorms
26-30	SW	Crossing Seas	29.75	Rain
31-35	W	Boarding Seas	29.50	Fog
35-40	NW	Tide Rips	29.25	Storm
_____other	Variable		29.00	Haze

Time	Notes

Time	Pilotage	Course	Speed	Log	Miles	Comments from the Helm
						Date: Day:
						From: To:
						Page

Morning Checklist		
Check	Comment	Initial
Engine Oil		
Coolant		
Battery Water		
Battery Condition #1		
Battery Condition #2		
Transmission		
Engine Hours		
Fuel		
Water Tank		
Holding Tank		
Pumps/Bilge		
Seacocks		
Radio and Electronics		
Radio and Electronics		

Crew and Guests

Wind Force	Wind Direction	Sea State	Barometer	Forecast
0-5	N	Glassy	31.00	Fair
6-10	NE	Small Chop	30.75	Rising Wind
11-15	E	Moderate Chop	30.50	Veering Wind
16-20	SE	Heavy Chop	30.25	Backing Wind
21-25	S	Ground Swell	30.00	Squalls/Thunderstorms
26-30	SW	Crossing Seas	29.75	Rain
31-35	W	Boarding Seas	29.50	Fog
35-40	NW	Tide Rips	29.25	Storm
_____other	Variable		29.00	Haze

Time	Notes

Time			Pilotage	Course	Speed	Log	Miles	Comments from the Helm
								Date: Day:
								From: To:
								Page

Morning Checklist			

Check		Comment	Initial
Engine Oil			
Coolant			
Battery Water			
Battery Condition	#1		
	#2		
Transmission			
Engine Hours			
Fuel			
Water Tank			
Holding Tank			
Pumps/Bilge			
Seacocks			
Radio and Electronics			

Crew and Guests			

Wind Force	Wind Direction	Sea State	Barometer	Forecast
0-5	N	Glassy	31.00	Fair
6-10	NE	Small Chop	30.75	Rising Wind
11-15	E	Moderate Chop	30.50	Veering Wind
16-20	SE	Heavy Chop	30.25	Backing Wind
21-25	S	Ground Swell	30.00	Squalls/Thunderstorms
26-30	SW	Crossing Seas	29.75	Rain
31-35	W	Boarding Seas	29.50	Fog
35-40	NW	Tide Rips	29.25	Storm
____other	Variable		29.00	Haze

Time	Notes

Time	Pilotage		Course	Speed	Log	Miles	Comments from the Helm		
									Date:
									Day:
								From:	
								To:	
								Page	

Morning Checklist		
Check	Comment	Initial
Engine Oil		
Coolant		
Battery Water		
Battery Condition #1		
Battery Condition #2		
Transmission		
Engine Hours		
Fuel		
Water Tank		
Holding Tank		
Pumps/Bilge		
Seacocks		
Radio and Electronics		

Crew and Guests

Wind Force	Wind Direction	Sea State	Barometer	Forecast
0-5	N	Glassy	31.00	Fair
6-10	NE	Small Chop	30.75	Rising Wind
11-15	E	Moderate Chop	30.50	Veering Wind
16-20	SE	Heavy Chop	30.25	Backing Wind
21-25	S	Ground Swell	30.00	Squalls/Thunderstorms
26-30	SW	Crossing Seas	29.75	Rain
31-35	W	Boarding Seas	29.50	Fog
35-40	NW	Tide Rips	29.25	Storm
_____other	Variable		29.00	Haze

Time	Notes

Time			Pilotage	Course	Speed	Log	Miles	Comments from the Helm		
									Date:	Day:
									From:	To:
									Page	

Morning Checklist		
Check	Comment	Initial
Engine Oil		
Coolant		
Battery Water		
Battery Condition #1		
Battery Condition #2		
Transmission		
Engine Hours		
Fuel		
Water Tank		
Holding Tank		
Pumps/Bilge		
Seacocks		
Radio and Electronics		

Crew and Guests		

Wind Force	Wind Direction	Sea State	Barometer	Forecast
0-5	N	Glassy	31.00	Fair
6-10	NE	Small Chop	30.75	Rising Wind
11-15	E	Moderate Chop	30.50	Veering Wind
16-20	SE	Heavy Chop	30.25	Backing Wind
21-25	S	Ground Swell	30.00	Squalls/Thunderstorms
26-30	SW	Crossing Seas	29.75	Rain
31-35	W	Boarding Seas	29.50	Fog
35-40	NW	Tide Rips	29.25	Storm
_____other	Variable		29.00	Haze

Time	Notes

Time	Pilotage	Course	Speed	Log	Miles	Comments from the Helm
						Date: Day:
						From: To:
						Page

Morning Checklist		
Check	Comment	Initial
Engine Oil		
Coolant		
Battery Water		
Battery Condition #1		
Battery Condition #2		
Transmission		
Engine Hours		
Fuel		
Water Tank		
Holding Tank		
Pumps/Bilge		
Seacocks		
Radio and Electronics		

Crew and Guests

Wind Force	Wind Direction	Sea State	Barometer	Forecast
0-5	N	Glassy	31.00	Fair
6-10	NE	Small Chop	30.75	Rising Wind
11-15	E	Moderate Chop	30.50	Veering Wind
16-20	SE	Heavy Chop	30.25	Backing Wind
21-25	S	Ground Swell	30.00	Squalls/Thunderstorms
26-30	SW	Crossing Seas	29.75	Rain
31-35	W	Boarding Seas	29.50	Fog
35-40	NW	Tide Rips	29.25	Storm
_____other	Variable		29.00	Haze

Time	Notes

Time	Pilotage	Course	Speed	Log	Miles	Comments from the Helm
						Date:
						Day:
						From:
						To:
						Page

Morning Checklist		
Check	Comment	Initial
Engine Oil		
Coolant		
Battery Water		
Battery Condition #1		
#2		
Transmission		
Engine Hours		
Fuel		
Water Tank		
Holding Tank		
Pumps/Bilge		
Seacocks		
Radio and Electronics		

Crew and Guests

Wind Force	Wind Direction	Sea State	Barometer	Forecast
0-5	N	Glassy	31.00	Fair
6-10	NE	Small Chop	30.75	Rising Wind
11-15	E	Moderate Chop	30.50	Veering Wind
16-20	SE	Heavy Chop	30.25	Backing Wind
21-25	S	Ground Swell	30.00	Squalls/Thunderstorms
26-30	SW	Crossing Seas	29.75	Rain
31-35	W	Boarding Seas	29.50	Fog
35-40	NW	Tide Rips	29.25	Storm
_____other	Variable		29.00	Haze

Time	Notes

Time			Pilotage	Course	Speed	Log	Miles	Comments from the Helm		
										Date:
									Day:	
									To:	From:
									Page	

Morning Checklist		
Check	Comment	Initial
Engine Oil		
Coolant		
Battery Water		
Battery Condition #1		
Battery Condition #2		
Transmission		
Engine Hours		
Fuel		
Water Tank		
Holding Tank		
Pumps/Bilge		
Seacocks		
Radio and Electronics		
Crew and Guests		

Wind Force	Wind Direction	Sea State	Barometer	Forecast
0-5	N	Glassy	31.00	Fair
6-10	NE	Small Chop	30.75	Rising Wind
11-15	E	Moderate Chop	30.50	Veering Wind
16-20	SE	Heavy Chop	30.25	Backing Wind
21-25	S	Ground Swell	30.00	Squalls/Thunderstorms
26-30	SW	Crossing Seas	29.75	Rain
31-35	W	Boarding Seas	29.50	Fog
35-40	NW	Tide Rips	29.25	Storm
_____other	Variable		29.00	Haze

Time	Notes

Time	Pilotage	Course	Speed	Log	Miles	Comments from the Helm
						Date:
						Day:
						From:
						To:
						Page

Morning Checklist		
Check	Comment	Initial
Engine Oil		
Coolant		
Battery Water		
Battery Condition #1		
Battery Condition #2		
Transmission		
Engine Hours		
Fuel		
Water Tank		
Holding Tank		
Pumps/Bilge		
Seacocks		
Radio and Electronics		

Crew and Guests

Wind Force	Wind Direction	Sea State	Barometer	Forecast
0-5	N	Glassy	31.00	Fair
6-10	NE	Small Chop	30.75	Rising Wind
11-15	E	Moderate Chop	30.50	Veering Wind
16-20	SE	Heavy Chop	30.25	Backing Wind
21-25	S	Ground Swell	30.00	Squalls/Thunderstorms
26-30	SW	Crossing Seas	29.75	Rain
31-35	W	Boarding Seas	29.50	Fog
35-40	NW	Tide Rips	29.25	Storm
____other	Variable		29.00	Haze

Time	Notes

Time			Pilotage	Course	Speed	Log	Miles	Comments from the Helm		
										Date:
									Day:	
									To:	From:
									Page	

Morning Checklist		
Check	Comment	Initial
Engine Oil		
Coolant		
Battery Water		
Battery Condition #1		
Battery Condition #2		
Transmission		
Engine Hours		
Fuel		
Water Tank		
Holding Tank		
Pumps/Bilge		
Seacocks		
Radio and Electronics		

Crew and Guests

Wind Force	Wind Direction	Sea State	Barometer	Forecast
0-5	N	Glassy	31.00	Fair
6-10	NE	Small Chop	30.75	Rising Wind
11-15	E	Moderate Chop	30.50	Veering Wind
16-20	SE	Heavy Chop	30.25	Backing Wind
21-25	S	Ground Swell	30.00	Squalls/Thunderstorms
26-30	SW	Crossing Seas	29.75	Rain
31-35	W	Boarding Seas	29.50	Fog
35-40	NW	Tide Rips	29.25	Storm
_____other	Variable		29.00	Haze

Time	Notes

Time		Pilotage	Course	Speed	Log	Miles	Comments from the Helm
							Date:
							Day:
							From:
							To:
							Page

Morning Checklist

Check		Comment	Initial
Engine Oil			
Coolant			
Battery Water			
Battery Condition	#1		
	#2		
Transmission			
Engine Hours			
Fuel			
Water Tank			
Holding Tank			
Pumps/Bilge			
Seacocks			
Radio and Electronics			

Crew and Guests

Wind Force	Wind Direction	Sea State	Barometer	Forecast
0-5	N	Glassy	31.00	Fair
6-10	NE	Small Chop	30.75	Rising Wind
11-15	E	Moderate Chop	30.50	Veering Wind
16-20	SE	Heavy Chop	30.25	Backing Wind
21-25	S	Ground Swell	30.00	Squalls/Thunderstorms
26-30	SW	Crossing Seas	29.75	Rain
31-35	W	Boarding Seas	29.50	Fog
35-40	NW	Tide Rips	29.25	Storm
_____other	Variable		29.00	Haze

Time	Notes

Time	Pilotage	Course	Speed	Log	Miles	Comments from the Helm
						Date: Day:
						From: To:
						Page

Morning Checklist

Check	Comment	Initial
Engine Oil		
Coolant		
Battery Water		
Battery Condition #1		
Battery Condition #2		
Transmission		
Engine Hours		
Fuel		
Water Tank		
Holding Tank		
Pumps/Bilge		
Seacocks		
Radio and Electronics		

Crew and Guests

Wind Force	Wind Direction	Sea State	Barometer	Forecast
0-5	N	Glassy	31.00	Fair
6-10	NE	Small Chop	30.75	Rising Wind
11-15	E	Moderate Chop	30.50	Veering Wind
16-20	SE	Heavy Chop	30.25	Backing Wind
21-25	S	Ground Swell	30.00	Squalls/Thunderstorms
26-30	SW	Crossing Seas	29.75	Rain
31-35	W	Boarding Seas	29.50	Fog
35-40	NW	Tide Rips	29.25	Storm
_____other	Variable		29.00	Haze

Time	Notes

Time	Pilotage	Course	Speed	Log	Miles	Comments from the Helm
						Date: Day:
						From: To:
						Page

Morning Checklist

Check		Comment	Initial
Engine Oil			
Coolant			
Battery Water			
Battery Condition	#1		
	#2		
Transmission			
Engine Hours			
Fuel			
Water Tank			
Holding Tank			
Pumps/Bilge			
Seacocks			
Radio and Electronics			

Crew and Guests

Wind Force	Wind Direction	Sea State	Barometer	Forecast
0-5	N	Glassy	31.00	Fair
6-10	NE	Small Chop	30.75	Rising Wind
11-15	E	Moderate Chop	30.50	Veering Wind
16-20	SE	Heavy Chop	30.25	Backing Wind
21-25	S	Ground Swell	30.00	Squalls/Thunderstorms
26-30	SW	Crossing Seas	29.75	Rain
31-35	W	Boarding Seas	29.50	Fog
35-40	NW	Tide Rips	29.25	Storm
_____other	Variable		29.00	Haze

Time	Notes

Time	Pilotage		Course	Speed	Log	Miles	Comments from the Helm
							Date:
							Day:
							From:
							To:
							Page

Morning Checklist		
Check	Comment	Initial
Engine Oil		
Coolant		
Battery Water		
Battery Condition #1		
Battery Condition #2		
Transmission		
Engine Hours		
Fuel		
Water Tank		
Holding Tank		
Pumps/Bilge		
Seacocks		
Radio and Electronics		

Crew and Guests

Wind Force	Wind Direction	Sea State	Barometer	Forecast
0-5	N	Glassy	31.00	Fair
6-10	NE	Small Chop	30.75	Rising Wind
11-15	E	Moderate Chop	30.50	Veering Wind
16-20	SE	Heavy Chop	30.25	Backing Wind
21-25	S	Ground Swell	30.00	Squalls/Thunderstorms
26-30	SW	Crossing Seas	29.75	Rain
31-35	W	Boarding Seas	29.50	Fog
35-40	NW	Tide Rips	29.25	Storm
_____other	Variable		29.00	Haze

Time	Notes

Time			Pilotage	Course	Speed	Log	Miles	Comments from the Helm		
										Date:
									Day:	
										From:
									To:	
									Page	

Morning Checklist		
Check	Comment	Initial
Engine Oil		
Coolant		
Battery Water		
Battery Condition #1		
Battery Condition #2		
Transmission		
Engine Hours		
Fuel		
Water Tank		
Holding Tank		
Pumps/Bilge		
Seacocks		
Radio and Electronics		
Radio and Electronics		
Radio and Electronics		

Crew and Guests

Wind Force	Wind Direction	Sea State	Barometer	Forecast
0-5	N	Glassy	31.00	Fair
6-10	NE	Small Chop	30.75	Rising Wind
11-15	E	Moderate Chop	30.50	Veering Wind
16-20	SE	Heavy Chop	30.25	Backing Wind
21-25	S	Ground Swell	30.00	Squalls/Thunderstorms
26-30	SW	Crossing Seas	29.75	Rain
31-35	W	Boarding Seas	29.50	Fog
35-40	NW	Tide Rips	29.25	Storm
_____other	Variable		29.00	Haze

Time	Notes

Time			Pilotage	Course	Speed	Log	Miles	Comments from the Helm
								Date: Day:
								From: To:
								Page

Morning Checklist		
Check	**Comment**	**Initial**
Engine Oil		
Coolant		
Battery Water		
Battery Condition #1		
Battery Condition #2		
Transmission		
Engine Hours		
Fuel		
Water Tank		
Holding Tank		
Pumps/Bilge		
Seacocks		
Radio and Electronics		

Crew and Guests

Wind Force	Wind Direction	Sea State	Barometer	Forecast
0-5	N	Glassy	31.00	Fair
6-10	NE	Small Chop	30.75	Rising Wind
11-15	E	Moderate Chop	30.50	Veering Wind
16-20	SE	Heavy Chop	30.25	Backing Wind
21-25	S	Ground Swell	30.00	Squalls/Thunderstorms
26-30	SW	Crossing Seas	29.75	Rain
31-35	W	Boarding Seas	29.50	Fog
35-40	NW	Tide Rips	29.25	Storm
_____other	Variable		29.00	Haze

Time	Notes

Time	Pilotage	Course	Speed	Log	Miles	Comments from the Helm
						Date: Day:
						From: To:
						Page

Morning Checklist		
Check	Comment	Initial
Engine Oil		
Coolant		
Battery Water		
Battery Condition #1		
Battery Condition #2		
Transmission		
Engine Hours		
Fuel		
Water Tank		
Holding Tank		
Pumps/Bilge		
Seacocks		
Radio and Electronics		

Crew and Guests

Wind Force	Wind Direction	Sea State	Barometer	Forecast
0-5	N	Glassy	31.00	Fair
6-10	NE	Small Chop	30.75	Rising Wind
11-15	E	Moderate Chop	30.50	Veering Wind
16-20	SE	Heavy Chop	30.25	Backing Wind
21-25	S	Ground Swell	30.00	Squalls/Thunderstorms
26-30	SW	Crossing Seas	29.75	Rain
31-35	W	Boarding Seas	29.50	Fog
35-40	NW	Tide Rips	29.25	Storm
_____other	Variable		29.00	Haze

Time	Notes

Time		Pilotage	Course	Speed	Log	Miles	Comments from the Helm		
									Date:
								Day:	
								To:	From:
								Page	

Morning Checklist

Check		Comment	Initial
Engine Oil			
Coolant			
Battery Water			
Battery Condition	#1		
	#2		
Transmission			
Engine Hours			
Fuel			
Water Tank			
Holding Tank			
Pumps/Bilge			
Seacocks			
Radio and Electronics			

Crew and Guests

Wind Force	Wind Direction	Sea State	Barometer	Forecast
0-5	N	Glassy	31.00	Fair
6-10	NE	Small Chop	30.75	Rising Wind
11-15	E	Moderate Chop	30.50	Veering Wind
16-20	SE	Heavy Chop	30.25	Backing Wind
21-25	S	Ground Swell	30.00	Squalls/Thunderstorms
26-30	SW	Crossing Seas	29.75	Rain
31-35	W	Boarding Seas	29.50	Fog
35-40	NW	Tide Rips	29.25	Storm
_____other	Variable		29.00	Haze

Time	Notes

Time	Pilotage		Course	Speed	Log	Miles	Comments from the Helm
							Date: Day:
							From: To:
							Page

Morning Checklist

Check		Comment	Initial
Engine Oil			
Coolant			
Battery Water			
Battery Condition	#1		
	#2		
Transmission			
Engine Hours			
Fuel			
Water Tank			
Holding Tank			
Pumps/Bilge			
Seacocks			
Radio and Electronics			

Crew and Guests

Wind Force	Wind Direction	Sea State	Barometer	Forecast
0-5	N	Glassy	31.00	Fair
6-10	NE	Small Chop	30.75	Rising Wind
11-15	E	Moderate Chop	30.50	Veering Wind
16-20	SE	Heavy Chop	30.25	Backing Wind
21-25	S	Ground Swell	30.00	Squalls/Thunderstorms
26-30	SW	Crossing Seas	29.75	Rain
31-35	W	Boarding Seas	29.50	Fog
35-40	NW	Tide Rips	29.25	Storm
_____other	Variable		29.00	Haze

Time	Notes

Time		Pilotage	Course	Speed	Log	Miles	Comments from the Helm		
								Day:	Date:
									To:	From:
								Page	

Morning Checklist		
Check	Comment	Initial
Engine Oil		
Coolant		
Battery Water		
Battery Condition #1		
Battery Condition #2		
Transmission		
Engine Hours		
Fuel		
Water Tank		
Holding Tank		
Pumps/Bilge		
Seacocks		
Radio and Electronics		

Crew and Guests		

Wind Force	Wind Direction	Sea State	Barometer	Forecast
0-5	N	Glassy	31.00	Fair
6-10	NE	Small Chop	30.75	Rising Wind
11-15	E	Moderate Chop	30.50	Veering Wind
16-20	SE	Heavy Chop	30.25	Backing Wind
21-25	S	Ground Swell	30.00	Squalls/Thunderstorms
26-30	SW	Crossing Seas	29.75	Rain
31-35	W	Boarding Seas	29.50	Fog
35-40	NW	Tide Rips	29.25	Storm
_____other	Variable		29.00	Haze

Time	Notes

Time	Pilotage	Course	Speed	Log	Miles	Comments from the Helm
						Date: / Day:
						From: / To:
						Page

Morning Checklist			

Check		Comment	Initial
Engine Oil			
Coolant			
Battery Water			
Battery Condition	#1		
	#2		
Transmission			
Engine Hours			
Fuel			
Water Tank			
Holding Tank			
Pumps/Bilge			
Seacocks			
Radio and Electronics			

Crew and Guests

Wind Force	Wind Direction	Sea State	Barometer	Forecast
0-5	N	Glassy	31.00	Fair
6-10	NE	Small Chop	30.75	Rising Wind
11-15	E	Moderate Chop	30.50	Veering Wind
16-20	SE	Heavy Chop	30.25	Backing Wind
21-25	S	Ground Swell	30.00	Squalls/Thunderstorms
26-30	SW	Crossing Seas	29.75	Rain
31-35	W	Boarding Seas	29.50	Fog
35-40	NW	Tide Rips	29.25	Storm
_____other	Variable		29.00	Haze

Time	Notes

Time	Pilotage	Course	Speed	Log	Miles	Comments from the Helm
						Date: Day:
						From: To:
						Page

Morning Checklist

Check		Comment	Initial
Engine Oil			
Coolant			
Battery Water			
Battery Condition	#1		
	#2		
Transmission			
Engine Hours			
Fuel			
Water Tank			
Holding Tank			
Pumps/Bilge			
Seacocks			
Radio and Electronics			

Crew and Guests

Wind Force	Wind Direction	Sea State	Barometer	Forecast
0-5	N	Glassy	31.00	Fair
6-10	NE	Small Chop	30.75	Rising Wind
11-15	E	Moderate Chop	30.50	Veering Wind
16-20	SE	Heavy Chop	30.25	Backing Wind
21-25	S	Ground Swell	30.00	Squalls/Thunderstorms
26-30	SW	Crossing Seas	29.75	Rain
31-35	W	Boarding Seas	29.50	Fog
35-40	NW	Tide Rips	29.25	Storm
_____other	Variable		29.00	Haze

Time	Notes

Time			Pilotage	Course	Speed	Log	Miles	Comments from the Helm		
									Date:	
										Day:
									From:	
										To:
									Page	

Morning Checklist		

Check	Comment	Initial
Engine Oil		
Coolant		
Battery Water		
Battery Condition #1		
Battery Condition #2		
Transmission		
Engine Hours		
Fuel		
Water Tank		
Holding Tank		
Pumps/Bilge		
Seacocks		
Radio and Electronics		

Crew and Guests

Wind Force	Wind Direction	Sea State	Barometer	Forecast
0-5	N	Glassy	31.00	Fair
6-10	NE	Small Chop	30.75	Rising Wind
11-15	E	Moderate Chop	30.50	Veering Wind
16-20	SE	Heavy Chop	30.25	Backing Wind
21-25	S	Ground Swell	30.00	Squalls/Thunderstorms
26-30	SW	Crossing Seas	29.75	Rain
31-35	W	Boarding Seas	29.50	Fog
35-40	NW	Tide Rips	29.25	Storm
_____other	Variable		29.00	Haze

Time	Notes

Time		Pilotage	Course	Speed	Log	Miles	Comments from the Helm
							Date: Day:
							From: To:
							Page

Morning Checklist		
Check	**Comment**	**Initial**
Engine Oil		
Coolant		
Battery Water		
Battery Condition #1		
Battery Condition #2		
Transmission		
Engine Hours		
Fuel		
Water Tank		
Holding Tank		
Pumps/Bilge		
Seacocks		
Radio and Electronics		

Crew and Guests

Wind Force	Wind Direction	Sea State	Barometer	Forecast
0-5	N	Glassy	31.00	Fair
6-10	NE	Small Chop	30.75	Rising Wind
11-15	E	Moderate Chop	30.50	Veering Wind
16-20	SE	Heavy Chop	30.25	Backing Wind
21-25	S	Ground Swell	30.00	Squalls/Thunderstorms
26-30	SW	Crossing Seas	29.75	Rain
31-35	W	Boarding Seas	29.50	Fog
35-40	NW	Tide Rips	29.25	Storm
_____other	Variable		29.00	Haze

Time	Notes

Time			Pilotage	Course	Speed	Log	Miles	Comments from the Helm
								Date:
								Day:
								From:
								To:
								Page

Morning Checklist		
Check	Comment	Initial
Engine Oil		
Coolant		
Battery Water		
Battery Condition #1		
Battery Condition #2		
Transmission		
Engine Hours		
Fuel		
Water Tank		
Holding Tank		
Pumps/Bilge		
Seacocks		
Radio and Electronics		

Crew and Guests

Wind Force	Wind Direction	Sea State	Barometer	Forecast
0-5	N	Glassy	31.00	Fair
6-10	NE	Small Chop	30.75	Rising Wind
11-15	E	Moderate Chop	30.50	Veering Wind
16-20	SE	Heavy Chop	30.25	Backing Wind
21-25	S	Ground Swell	30.00	Squalls/Thunderstorms
26-30	SW	Crossing Seas	29.75	Rain
31-35	W	Boarding Seas	29.50	Fog
35-40	NW	Tide Rips	29.25	Storm
_____ other	Variable		29.00	Haze

Time	Notes

Time	Pilotage	Course	Speed	Log	Miles	Comments from the Helm
						Date: Day:
						From: To:
						Page

Morning Checklist

Check		Comment	Initial
Engine Oil			
Coolant			
Battery Water			
Battery Condition	#1		
	#2		
Transmission			
Engine Hours			
Fuel			
Water Tank			
Holding Tank			
Pumps/Bilge			
Seacocks			
Radio and Electronics			

Crew and Guests

Wind Force	Wind Direction	Sea State	Barometer	Forecast
0-5	N	Glassy	31.00	Fair
6-10	NE	Small Chop	30.75	Rising Wind
11-15	E	Moderate Chop	30.50	Veering Wind
16-20	SE	Heavy Chop	30.25	Backing Wind
21-25	S	Ground Swell	30.00	Squalls/Thunderstorms
26-30	SW	Crossing Seas	29.75	Rain
31-35	W	Boarding Seas	29.50	Fog
35-40	NW	Tide Rips	29.25	Storm
_____ other	Variable		29.00	Haze

Time	Notes

Time	Pilotage	Course	Speed	Log	Miles	Comments from the Helm
						Date:
						Day:
						From:
						To:
						Page

Morning Checklist		
Check	Comment	Initial
Engine Oil		
Coolant		
Battery Water		
Battery Condition	#1	
	#2	
Transmission		
Engine Hours		
Fuel		
Water Tank		
Holding Tank		
Pumps/Bilge		
Seacocks		
Radio and Electronics		

Crew and Guests

Wind Force	Wind Direction	Sea State	Barometer	Forecast
0-5	N	Glassy	31.00	Fair
6-10	NE	Small Chop	30.75	Rising Wind
11-15	E	Moderate Chop	30.50	Veering Wind
16-20	SE	Heavy Chop	30.25	Backing Wind
21-25	S	Ground Swell	30.00	Squalls/Thunderstorms
26-30	SW	Crossing Seas	29.75	Rain
31-35	W	Boarding Seas	29.50	Fog
35-40	NW	Tide Rips	29.25	Storm
_____other	Variable		29.00	Haze

Time	Notes

Time			Pilotage	Course	Speed	Log	Miles	Comments from the Helm
								Date:
								Day:
								From:
								To:
								Page

Morning Checklist		
Check	Comment	Initial
Engine Oil		
Coolant		
Battery Water		
Battery Condition #1		
Battery Condition #2		
Transmission		
Engine Hours		
Fuel		
Water Tank		
Holding Tank		
Pumps/Bilge		
Seacocks		
Radio and Electronics		

Crew and Guests

Wind Force	Wind Direction	Sea State	Barometer	Forecast
0-5	N	Glassy	31.00	Fair
6-10	NE	Small Chop	30.75	Rising Wind
11-15	E	Moderate Chop	30.50	Veering Wind
16-20	SE	Heavy Chop	30.25	Backing Wind
21-25	S	Ground Swell	30.00	Squalls/Thunderstorms
26-30	SW	Crossing Seas	29.75	Rain
31-35	W	Boarding Seas	29.50	Fog
35-40	NW	Tide Rips	29.25	Storm
_____other	Variable		29.00	Haze

Time	Notes

Time	Pilotage	Course	Speed	Log	Miles	Comments from the Helm

Date:

Day:

From:

To:

Page

Morning Checklist		
Check	Comment	Initial
Engine Oil		
Coolant		
Battery Water		
Battery Condition #1		
Battery Condition #2		
Transmission		
Engine Hours		
Fuel		
Water Tank		
Holding Tank		
Pumps/Bilge		
Seacocks		
Radio and Electronics		

Crew and Guests

Wind Force	Wind Direction	Sea State	Barometer	Forecast
0-5	N	Glassy	31.00	Fair
6-10	NE	Small Chop	30.75	Rising Wind
11-15	E	Moderate Chop	30.50	Veering Wind
16-20	SE	Heavy Chop	30.25	Backing Wind
21-25	S	Ground Swell	30.00	Squalls/Thunderstorms
26-30	SW	Crossing Seas	29.75	Rain
31-35	W	Boarding Seas	29.50	Fog
35-40	NW	Tide Rips	29.25	Storm
____other	Variable		29.00	Haze

Time	Notes

Time	Pilotage		Course	Speed	Log	Miles	Comments from the Helm

Date:

Day:

From:

To:

Page

Morning Checklist		
Check	Comment	Initial
Engine Oil		
Coolant		
Battery Water		
Battery Condition #1		
Battery Condition #2		
Transmission		
Engine Hours		
Fuel		
Water Tank		
Holding Tank		
Pumps/Bilge		
Seacocks		
Radio and Electronics		

Crew and Guests

Wind Force	Wind Direction	Sea State	Barometer	Forecast
0-5	N	Glassy	31.00	Fair
6-10	NE	Small Chop	30.75	Rising Wind
11-15	E	Moderate Chop	30.50	Veering Wind
16-20	SE	Heavy Chop	30.25	Backing Wind
21-25	S	Ground Swell	30.00	Squalls/Thunderstorms
26-30	SW	Crossing Seas	29.75	Rain
31-35	W	Boarding Seas	29.50	Fog
35-40	NW	Tide Rips	29.25	Storm
_____other	Variable		29.00	Haze

Time	Notes

Time	Pilotage	Course	Speed	Log	Miles	Comments from the Helm
						Date: Day:
						From: To:
						Page

Morning Checklist

Check		Comment	Initial
Engine Oil			
Coolant			
Battery Water			
Battery Condition	#1		
	#2		
Transmission			
Engine Hours			
Fuel			
Water Tank			
Holding Tank			
Pumps/Bilge			
Seacocks			
Radio and Electronics			

Crew and Guests

Wind Force	Wind Direction	Sea State	Barometer	Forecast
0-5	N	Glassy	31.00	Fair
6-10	NE	Small Chop	30.75	Rising Wind
11-15	E	Moderate Chop	30.50	Veering Wind
16-20	SE	Heavy Chop	30.25	Backing Wind
21-25	S	Ground Swell	30.00	Squalls/Thunderstorms
26-30	SW	Crossing Seas	29.75	Rain
31-35	W	Boarding Seas	29.50	Fog
35-40	NW	Tide Rips	29.25	Storm
_____other	Variable		29.00	Haze

Time	Notes

Time			Pilotage	Course	Speed	Log	Miles	Comments from the Helm
								Date:
								Day:
								From:
								To:
								Page

Morning Checklist		
Check	Comment	Initial
Engine Oil		
Coolant		
Battery Water		
Battery Condition #1		
Battery Condition #2		
Transmission		
Engine Hours		
Fuel		
Water Tank		
Holding Tank		
Pumps/Bilge		
Seacocks		
Radio and Electronics		

Crew and Guests

Wind Force	Wind Direction	Sea State	Barometer	Forecast
0-5	N	Glassy	31.00	Fair
6-10	NE	Small Chop	30.75	Rising Wind
11-15	E	Moderate Chop	30.50	Veering Wind
16-20	SE	Heavy Chop	30.25	Backing Wind
21-25	S	Ground Swell	30.00	Squalls/Thunderstorms
26-30	SW	Crossing Seas	29.75	Rain
31-35	W	Boarding Seas	29.50	Fog
35-40	NW	Tide Rips	29.25	Storm
_____other	Variable		29.00	Haze

Time	Notes

Time		Pilotage	Course	Speed	Log	Miles	Comments from the Helm
							Date: Day:
							From: To:
							Page

Morning Checklist		
Check	Comment	Initial
Engine Oil		
Coolant		
Battery Water		
Battery Condition #1		
Battery Condition #2		
Transmission		
Engine Hours		
Fuel		
Water Tank		
Holding Tank		
Pumps/Bilge		
Seacocks		
Radio and Electronics		

Crew and Guests

Wind Force	Wind Direction	Sea State	Barometer	Forecast
0-5	N	Glassy	31.00	Fair
6-10	NE	Small Chop	30.75	Rising Wind
11-15	E	Moderate Chop	30.50	Veering Wind
16-20	SE	Heavy Chop	30.25	Backing Wind
21-25	S	Ground Swell	30.00	Squalls/Thunderstorms
26-30	SW	Crossing Seas	29.75	Rain
31-35	W	Boarding Seas	29.50	Fog
35-40	NW	Tide Rips	29.25	Storm
_____other	Variable		29.00	Haze

Time	Notes

Time	Pilotage	Course	Speed	Log	Miles	Comments from the Helm
						Date: Day:
						From: To:
						Page

Morning Checklist		
Check	Comment	Initial
Engine Oil		
Coolant		
Battery Water		
Battery Condition #1		
Battery Condition #2		
Transmission		
Engine Hours		
Fuel		
Water Tank		
Holding Tank		
Pumps/Bilge		
Seacocks		
Radio and Electronics		

Crew and Guests

Wind Force	Wind Direction	Sea State	Barometer	Forecast
0-5	N	Glassy	31.00	Fair
6-10	NE	Small Chop	30.75	Rising Wind
11-15	E	Moderate Chop	30.50	Veering Wind
16-20	SE	Heavy Chop	30.25	Backing Wind
21-25	S	Ground Swell	30.00	Squalls/Thunderstorms
26-30	SW	Crossing Seas	29.75	Rain
31-35	W	Boarding Seas	29.50	Fog
35-40	NW	Tide Rips	29.25	Storm
_____other	Variable		29.00	Haze

Time	Notes

Time		Pilotage	Course	Speed	Log	Miles	Comments from the Helm
							Date: Day:
							From: To:
							Page

Morning Checklist		
Check	Comment	Initial
Engine Oil		
Coolant		
Battery Water		
Battery Condition #1		
#2		
Transmission		
Engine Hours		
Fuel		
Water Tank		
Holding Tank		
Pumps/Bilge		
Seacocks		
Radio and Electronics		

Crew and Guests

Wind Force	Wind Direction	Sea State	Barometer	Forecast
0-5	N	Glassy	31.00	Fair
6-10	NE	Small Chop	30.75	Rising Wind
11-15	E	Moderate Chop	30.50	Veering Wind
16-20	SE	Heavy Chop	30.25	Backing Wind
21-25	S	Ground Swell	30.00	Squalls/Thunderstorms
26-30	SW	Crossing Seas	29.75	Rain
31-35	W	Boarding Seas	29.50	Fog
35-40	NW	Tide Rips	29.25	Storm
_____other	Variable		29.00	Haze

Time	Notes

Time	Pilotage	Course	Speed	Log	Miles	Comments from the Helm
						Date: Day:
						From: To:
						Page

Morning Checklist		
Check	Comment	Initial
Engine Oil		
Coolant		
Battery Water		
Battery Condition #1		
Battery Condition #2		
Transmission		
Engine Hours		
Fuel		
Water Tank		
Holding Tank		
Pumps/Bilge		
Seacocks		
Radio and Electronics		

Crew and Guests

Wind Force	Wind Direction	Sea State	Barometer	Forecast
0-5	N	Glassy	31.00	Fair
6-10	NE	Small Chop	30.75	Rising Wind
11-15	E	Moderate Chop	30.50	Veering Wind
16-20	SE	Heavy Chop	30.25	Backing Wind
21-25	S	Ground Swell	30.00	Squalls/Thunderstorms
26-30	SW	Crossing Seas	29.75	Rain
31-35	W	Boarding Seas	29.50	Fog
35-40	NW	Tide Rips	29.25	Storm
_____other	Variable		29.00	Haze

Time	Notes

Time		Pilotage	Course	Speed	Log	Miles	Comments from the Helm
							Date:
							Day:
							From:
							To:
							Page

Morning Checklist		
Check	Comment	Initial
Engine Oil		
Coolant		
Battery Water		
Battery Condition	#1	
	#2	
Transmission		
Engine Hours		
Fuel		
Water Tank		
Holding Tank		
Pumps/Bilge		
Seacocks		
Radio and Electronics		

Crew and Guests

Wind Force	Wind Direction	Sea State	Barometer	Forecast
0-5	N	Glassy	31.00	Fair
6-10	NE	Small Chop	30.75	Rising Wind
11-15	E	Moderate Chop	30.50	Veering Wind
16-20	SE	Heavy Chop	30.25	Backing Wind
21-25	S	Ground Swell	30.00	Squalls/Thunderstorms
26-30	SW	Crossing Seas	29.75	Rain
31-35	W	Boarding Seas	29.50	Fog
35-40	NW	Tide Rips	29.25	Storm
_____other	Variable		29.00	Haze

Time	Notes

Time		Pilotage	Course	Speed	Log	Miles	Comments from the Helm
							Date:
							Day:
							From:
							To:
							Page

Morning Checklist		
Check	Comment	Initial
Engine Oil		
Coolant		
Battery Water		
Battery Condition #1		
Battery Condition #2		
Transmission		
Engine Hours		
Fuel		
Water Tank		
Holding Tank		
Pumps/Bilge		
Seacocks		
Radio and Electronics		

Crew and Guests		

Wind Force	Wind Direction	Sea State	Barometer	Forecast
0-5	N	Glassy	31.00	Fair
6-10	NE	Small Chop	30.75	Rising Wind
11-15	E	Moderate Chop	30.50	Veering Wind
16-20	SE	Heavy Chop	30.25	Backing Wind
21-25	S	Ground Swell	30.00	Squalls/Thunderstorms
26-30	SW	Crossing Seas	29.75	Rain
31-35	W	Boarding Seas	29.50	Fog
35-40	NW	Tide Rips	29.25	Storm
_____other	Variable		29.00	Haze

Time	Notes

Time			Pilotage	Course	Speed	Log	Miles	Comments from the Helm	
									Date:
									Day:
									From:
									To:
									Page

Morning Checklist

Check		Comment	Initial
Engine Oil			
Coolant			
Battery Water			
Battery Condition	#1		
	#2		
Transmission			
Engine Hours			
Fuel			
Water Tank			
Holding Tank			
Pumps/Bilge			
Seacocks			
Radio and Electronics			

Crew and Guests

Wind Force	Wind Direction	Sea State	Barometer	Forecast
0-5	N	Glassy	31.00	Fair
6-10	NE	Small Chop	30.75	Rising Wind
11-15	E	Moderate Chop	30.50	Veering Wind
16-20	SE	Heavy Chop	30.25	Backing Wind
21-25	S	Ground Swell	30.00	Squalls/Thunderstorms
26-30	SW	Crossing Seas	29.75	Rain
31-35	W	Boarding Seas	29.50	Fog
35-40	NW	Tide Rips	29.25	Storm
_____other	Variable		29.00	Haze

Time	Notes

Time	Pilotage	Course	Speed	Log	Miles	Comments from the Helm
						Date:
						Day:
						From:
						To:
						Page

Morning Checklist

Check		Comment	Initial
Engine Oil			
Coolant			
Battery Water			
Battery Condition	#1		
	#2		
Transmission			
Engine Hours			
Fuel			
Water Tank			
Holding Tank			
Pumps/Bilge			
Seacocks			
Radio and Electronics			

Crew and Guests

Wind Force	Wind Direction	Sea State	Barometer	Forecast
0-5	N	Glassy	31.00	Fair
6-10	NE	Small Chop	30.75	Rising Wind
11-15	E	Moderate Chop	30.50	Veering Wind
16-20	SE	Heavy Chop	30.25	Backing Wind
21-25	S	Ground Swell	30.00	Squalls/Thunderstorms
26-30	SW	Crossing Seas	29.75	Rain
31-35	W	Boarding Seas	29.50	Fog
35-40	NW	Tide Rips	29.25	Storm
_____other	Variable		29.00	Haze

Time	Notes

Time		Pilotage	Course	Speed	Log	Miles	Comments from the Helm
							Date: Day:
							From: To:
							Page

Morning Checklist		
Check	Comment	Initial
Engine Oil		
Coolant		
Battery Water		
Battery Condition #1		
Battery Condition #2		
Transmission		
Engine Hours		
Fuel		
Water Tank		
Holding Tank		
Pumps/Bilge		
Seacocks		
Radio and Electronics		

Crew and Guests		

Wind Force	Wind Direction	Sea State	Barometer	Forecast
0-5	N	Glassy	31.00	Fair
6-10	NE	Small Chop	30.75	Rising Wind
11-15	E	Moderate Chop	30.50	Veering Wind
16-20	SE	Heavy Chop	30.25	Backing Wind
21-25	S	Ground Swell	30.00	Squalls/Thunderstorms
26-30	SW	Crossing Seas	29.75	Rain
31-35	W	Boarding Seas	29.50	Fog
35-40	NW	Tide Rips	29.25	Storm
_____other	Variable		29.00	Haze

Time	Notes

Time		Pilotage	Course	Speed	Log	Miles	Comments from the Helm	
								Date: Day:
								From: To:
								Page

Morning Checklist		
Check	Comment	Initial
Engine Oil		
Coolant		
Battery Water		
Battery Condition #1		
Battery Condition #2		
Transmission		
Engine Hours		
Fuel		
Water Tank		
Holding Tank		
Pumps/Bilge		
Seacocks		
Radio and Electronics		

Crew and Guests

Wind Force	Wind Direction	Sea State	Barometer	Forecast
0-5	N	Glassy	31.00	Fair
6-10	NE	Small Chop	30.75	Rising Wind
11-15	E	Moderate Chop	30.50	Veering Wind
16-20	SE	Heavy Chop	30.25	Backing Wind
21-25	S	Ground Swell	30.00	Squalls/Thunderstorms
26-30	SW	Crossing Seas	29.75	Rain
31-35	W	Boarding Seas	29.50	Fog
35-40	NW	Tide Rips	29.25	Storm
_____other	Variable		29.00	Haze

Time	Notes

Time	Pilotage	Course	Speed	Log	Miles	Comments from the Helm
						Date: Day:
						From: To:
						Page

Morning Checklist		
Check	Comment	Initial
Engine Oil		
Coolant		
Battery Water		
Battery Condition #1		
Battery Condition #2		
Transmission		
Engine Hours		
Fuel		
Water Tank		
Holding Tank		
Pumps/Bilge		
Seacocks		
Radio and Electronics		

Crew and Guests

Wind Force	Wind Direction	Sea State	Barometer	Forecast
0-5	N	Glassy	31.00	Fair
6-10	NE	Small Chop	30.75	Rising Wind
11-15	E	Moderate Chop	30.50	Veering Wind
16-20	SE	Heavy Chop	30.25	Backing Wind
21-25	S	Ground Swell	30.00	Squalls/Thunderstorms
26-30	SW	Crossing Seas	29.75	Rain
31-35	W	Boarding Seas	29.50	Fog
35-40	NW	Tide Rips	29.25	Storm
_____other	Variable		29.00	Haze

Time	Notes

Time		Pilotage	Course	Speed	Log	Miles	Comments from the Helm
							Date:
							Day:
							From:
							To:
							Page

Morning Checklist			
Check		Comment	Initial
Engine Oil			
Coolant			
Battery Water			
Battery Condition	#1		
	#2		
Transmission			
Engine Hours			
Fuel			
Water Tank			
Holding Tank			
Pumps/Bilge			
Seacocks			
Radio and Electronics			

Crew and Guests

Wind Force	Wind Direction	Sea State	Barometer	Forecast
0-5	N	Glassy	31.00	Fair
6-10	NE	Small Chop	30.75	Rising Wind
11-15	E	Moderate Chop	30.50	Veering Wind
16-20	SE	Heavy Chop	30.25	Backing Wind
21-25	S	Ground Swell	30.00	Squalls/Thunderstorms
26-30	SW	Crossing Seas	29.75	Rain
31-35	W	Boarding Seas	29.50	Fog
35-40	NW	Tide Rips	29.25	Storm
_____other	Variable		29.00	Haze

Time	Notes

Time	Pilotage		Course	Speed	Log	Miles	Comments from the Helm
							Date:
							Day:
							From:
							To:
							Page

Morning Checklist

Check		Comment	Initial
Engine Oil			
Coolant			
Battery Water			
Battery Condition	#1		
	#2		
Transmission			
Engine Hours			
Fuel			
Water Tank			
Holding Tank			
Pumps/Bilge			
Seacocks			
Radio and Electronics			

Crew and Guests

Wind Force	Wind Direction	Sea State	Barometer	Forecast
0-5	N	Glassy	31.00	Fair
6-10	NE	Small Chop	30.75	Rising Wind
11-15	E	Moderate Chop	30.50	Veering Wind
16-20	SE	Heavy Chop	30.25	Backing Wind
21-25	S	Ground Swell	30.00	Squalls/Thunderstorms
26-30	SW	Crossing Seas	29.75	Rain
31-35	W	Boarding Seas	29.50	Fog
35-40	NW	Tide Rips	29.25	Storm
_____other	Variable		29.00	Haze

Time	Notes

Time		Pilotage	Course	Speed	Log	Miles	Comments from the Helm		
									Date:
								Day:	
								To:	From:
								Page	

Morning Checklist		
Check	Comment	Initial
Engine Oil		
Coolant		
Battery Water		
Battery Condition #1		
Battery Condition #2		
Transmission		
Engine Hours		
Fuel		
Water Tank		
Holding Tank		
Pumps/Bilge		
Seacocks		
Radio and Electronics		

Crew and Guests

Wind Force	Wind Direction	Sea State	Barometer	Forecast
0-5	N	Glassy	31.00	Fair
6-10	NE	Small Chop	30.75	Rising Wind
11-15	E	Moderate Chop	30.50	Veering Wind
16-20	SE	Heavy Chop	30.25	Backing Wind
21-25	S	Ground Swell	30.00	Squalls/Thunderstorms
26-30	SW	Crossing Seas	29.75	Rain
31-35	W	Boarding Seas	29.50	Fog
35-40	NW	Tide Rips	29.25	Storm
_____other	Variable		29.00	Haze

Time	Notes

Time			Pilotage	Course	Speed	Log	Miles	Comments from the Helm		
									Date:	
										Day:
									From:	
										To:
									Page	

Morning Checklist		
Check	Comment	Initial
Engine Oil		
Coolant		
Battery Water		
Battery Condition #1		
Battery Condition #2		
Transmission		
Engine Hours		
Fuel		
Water Tank		
Holding Tank		
Pumps/Bilge		
Seacocks		
Radio and Electronics		

Crew and Guests

Wind Force	Wind Direction	Sea State	Barometer	Forecast
0-5	N	Glassy	31.00	Fair
6-10	NE	Small Chop	30.75	Rising Wind
11-15	E	Moderate Chop	30.50	Veering Wind
16-20	SE	Heavy Chop	30.25	Backing Wind
21-25	S	Ground Swell	30.00	Squalls/Thunderstorms
26-30	SW	Crossing Seas	29.75	Rain
31-35	W	Boarding Seas	29.50	Fog
35-40	NW	Tide Rips	29.25	Storm
_____other	Variable		29.00	Haze

Time	Notes

Time			Pilotage	Course	Speed	Log	Miles	Comments from the Helm
								Date:
								Day:
								From:
								To:
								Page

Morning Checklist		
Check	Comment	Initial
Engine Oil		
Coolant		
Battery Water		
Battery Condition #1		
Battery Condition #2		
Transmission		
Engine Hours		
Fuel		
Water Tank		
Holding Tank		
Pumps/Bilge		
Seacocks		
Radio and Electronics		

Crew and Guests

Wind Force	Wind Direction	Sea State	Barometer	Forecast
0-5	N	Glassy	31.00	Fair
6-10	NE	Small Chop	30.75	Rising Wind
11-15	E	Moderate Chop	30.50	Veering Wind
16-20	SE	Heavy Chop	30.25	Backing Wind
21-25	S	Ground Swell	30.00	Squalls/Thunderstorms
26-30	SW	Crossing Seas	29.75	Rain
31-35	W	Boarding Seas	29.50	Fog
35-40	NW	Tide Rips	29.25	Storm
_____other	Variable		29.00	Haze

Time	Notes

Time	Pilotage	Course	Speed	Log	Miles	Comments from the Helm
						Date: Day:
						From: To:
						Page

Morning Checklist		
Check	Comment	Initial
Engine Oil		
Coolant		
Battery Water		
Battery Condition #1		
Battery Condition #2		
Transmission		
Engine Hours		
Fuel		
Water Tank		
Holding Tank		
Pumps/Bilge		
Seacocks		
Radio and Electronics		
Crew and Guests		

Wind Force	Wind Direction	Sea State	Barometer	Forecast
0-5	N	Glassy	31.00	Fair
6-10	NE	Small Chop	30.75	Rising Wind
11-15	E	Moderate Chop	30.50	Veering Wind
16-20	SE	Heavy Chop	30.25	Backing Wind
21-25	S	Ground Swell	30.00	Squalls/Thunderstorms
26-30	SW	Crossing Seas	29.75	Rain
31-35	W	Boarding Seas	29.50	Fog
35-40	NW	Tide Rips	29.25	Storm
_____other	Variable		29.00	Haze

Time	Notes

Time	Pilotage		Course	Speed	Log	Miles	Comments from the Helm
							Date:
							Day:
							From:
							To:
							Page

Morning Checklist		
Check	Comment	Initial
Engine Oil		
Coolant		
Battery Water		
Battery Condition #1		
Battery Condition #2		
Transmission		
Engine Hours		
Fuel		
Water Tank		
Holding Tank		
Pumps/Bilge		
Seacocks		
Radio and Electronics		
Radio and Electronics		

Crew and Guests

Wind Force	Wind Direction	Sea State	Barometer	Forecast
0-5	N	Glassy	31.00	Fair
6-10	NE	Small Chop	30.75	Rising Wind
11-15	E	Moderate Chop	30.50	Veering Wind
16-20	SE	Heavy Chop	30.25	Backing Wind
21-25	S	Ground Swell	30.00	Squalls/Thunderstorms
26-30	SW	Crossing Seas	29.75	Rain
31-35	W	Boarding Seas	29.50	Fog
35-40	NW	Tide Rips	29.25	Storm
_____other	Variable		29.00	Haze

Time	Notes

Time		Pilotage	Course	Speed	Log	Miles	Comments from the Helm
							Date:
							Day:
							From:
							To:
							Page

Morning Checklist		
Check	Comment	Initial
Engine Oil		
Coolant		
Battery Water		
Battery Condition #1		
Battery Condition #2		
Transmission		
Engine Hours		
Fuel		
Water Tank		
Holding Tank		
Pumps/Bilge		
Seacocks		
Radio and Electronics		

Crew and Guests

Wind Force	Wind Direction	Sea State	Barometer	Forecast
0-5	N	Glassy	31.00	Fair
6-10	NE	Small Chop	30.75	Rising Wind
11-15	E	Moderate Chop	30.50	Veering Wind
16-20	SE	Heavy Chop	30.25	Backing Wind
21-25	S	Ground Swell	30.00	Squalls/Thunderstorms
26-30	SW	Crossing Seas	29.75	Rain
31-35	W	Boarding Seas	29.50	Fog
35-40	NW	Tide Rips	29.25	Storm
_____other	Variable		29.00	Haze

Time	Notes

Time	Pilotage	Course	Speed	Log	Miles	Comments from the Helm
						Date: / Day:
						From: / To:
						Page

Morning Checklist		
Check	Comment	Initial
Engine Oil		
Coolant		
Battery Water		
Battery Condition #1		
Battery Condition #2		
Transmission		
Engine Hours		
Fuel		
Water Tank		
Holding Tank		
Pumps/Bilge		
Seacocks		
Radio and Electronics		
Radio and Electronics		

Crew and Guests

Wind Force	Wind Direction	Sea State	Barometer	Forecast
0-5	N	Glassy	31.00	Fair
6-10	NE	Small Chop	30.75	Rising Wind
11-15	E	Moderate Chop	30.50	Veering Wind
16-20	SE	Heavy Chop	30.25	Backing Wind
21-25	S	Ground Swell	30.00	Squalls/Thunderstorms
26-30	SW	Crossing Seas	29.75	Rain
31-35	W	Boarding Seas	29.50	Fog
35-40	NW	Tide Rips	29.25	Storm
_____other	Variable		29.00	Haze

Time	Notes

Time		Pilotage	Course	Speed	Log	Miles	Comments from the Helm
							Date:
							Day:
							From:
							To:
							Page

Morning Checklist		
Check	Comment	Initial
Engine Oil		
Coolant		
Battery Water		
Battery Condition — #1		
Battery Condition — #2		
Transmission		
Engine Hours		
Fuel		
Water Tank		
Holding Tank		
Pumps/Bilge		
Seacocks		
Radio and Electronics		

Crew and Guests

Wind Force	Wind Direction	Sea State	Barometer	Forecast
0-5	N	Glassy	31.00	Fair
6-10	NE	Small Chop	30.75	Rising Wind
11-15	E	Moderate Chop	30.50	Veering Wind
16-20	SE	Heavy Chop	30.25	Backing Wind
21-25	S	Ground Swell	30.00	Squalls/Thunderstorms
26-30	SW	Crossing Seas	29.75	Rain
31-35	W	Boarding Seas	29.50	Fog
35-40	NW	Tide Rips	29.25	Storm
_____ other	Variable		29.00	Haze

Time	Notes

Time			Pilotage	Course	Speed	Log	Miles	Comments from the Helm
								Date:
								Day:
								From:
								To:
								Page

Morning Checklist		
Check	Comment	Initial
Engine Oil		
Coolant		
Battery Water		
Battery Condition #1		
Battery Condition #2		
Transmission		
Engine Hours		
Fuel		
Water Tank		
Holding Tank		
Pumps/Bilge		
Seacocks		
Radio and Electronics		
Radio and Electronics		

Crew and Guests

Wind Force	Wind Direction	Sea State	Barometer	Forecast
0-5	N	Glassy	31.00	Fair
6-10	NE	Small Chop	30.75	Rising Wind
11-15	E	Moderate Chop	30.50	Veering Wind
16-20	SE	Heavy Chop	30.25	Backing Wind
21-25	S	Ground Swell	30.00	Squalls/Thunderstorms
26-30	SW	Crossing Seas	29.75	Rain
31-35	W	Boarding Seas	29.50	Fog
35-40	NW	Tide Rips	29.25	Storm
_____other	Variable		29.00	Haze

Time	Notes

Time		Pilotage	Course	Speed	Log	Miles	Comments from the Helm
							Date:
							Day:
							From:
							To:
							Page

Morning Checklist

Check		Comment	Initial
Engine Oil			
Coolant			
Battery Water			
Battery Condition	#1		
	#2		
Transmission			
Engine Hours			
Fuel			
Water Tank			
Holding Tank			
Pumps/Bilge			
Seacocks			
Radio and Electronics			

Crew and Guests

Wind Force	Wind Direction	Sea State	Barometer	Forecast
0-5	N	Glassy	31.00	Fair
6-10	NE	Small Chop	30.75	Rising Wind
11-15	E	Moderate Chop	30.50	Veering Wind
16-20	SE	Heavy Chop	30.25	Backing Wind
21-25	S	Ground Swell	30.00	Squalls/Thunderstorms
26-30	SW	Crossing Seas	29.75	Rain
31-35	W	Boarding Seas	29.50	Fog
35-40	NW	Tide Rips	29.25	Storm
_____other	Variable		29.00	Haze

Time	Notes

Time			Pilotage	Course	Speed	Log	Miles	Comments from the Helm
								Date:
								Day:
								From:
								To:
								Page

Morning Checklist		
Check	Comment	Initial
Engine Oil		
Coolant		
Battery Water		
Battery Condition #1		
Battery Condition #2		
Transmission		
Engine Hours		
Fuel		
Water Tank		
Holding Tank		
Pumps/Bilge		
Seacocks		
Radio and Electronics		

Crew and Guests

Wind Force	Wind Direction	Sea State	Barometer	Forecast
0-5	N	Glassy	31.00	Fair
6-10	NE	Small Chop	30.75	Rising Wind
11-15	E	Moderate Chop	30.50	Veering Wind
16-20	SE	Heavy Chop	30.25	Backing Wind
21-25	S	Ground Swell	30.00	Squalls/Thunderstorms
26-30	SW	Crossing Seas	29.75	Rain
31-35	W	Boarding Seas	29.50	Fog
35-40	NW	Tide Rips	29.25	Storm
_____other	Variable		29.00	Haze

Time	Notes

Time	Pilotage	Course	Speed	Log	Miles	Comments from the Helm
						Date: Day:
						From: To:
						Page

		Morning Checklist		
Check		Comment		Initial
Engine Oil				
Coolant				
Battery Water				
Battery Condition	#1			
	#2			
Transmission				
Engine Hours				
Fuel				
Water Tank				
Holding Tank				
Pumps/Bilge				
Seacocks				
Radio and Electronics				

		Crew and Guests		

Wind Force	Wind Direction	Sea State	Barometer	Forecast
0-5	N	Glassy	31.00	Fair
6-10	NE	Small Chop	30.75	Rising Wind
11-15	E	Moderate Chop	30.50	Veering Wind
16-20	SE	Heavy Chop	30.25	Backing Wind
21-25	S	Ground Swell	30.00	Squalls/Thunderstorms
26-30	SW	Crossing Seas	29.75	Rain
31-35	W	Boarding Seas	29.50	Fog
35-40	NW	Tide Rips	29.25	Storm
_____other	Variable		29.00	Haze

Time	Notes

Time		Pilotage	Course	Speed	Log	Miles	Comments from the Helm		
									Date:
								Day:	
									From:
								To:	
								Page	

Morning Checklist		
Check	Comment	Initial
Engine Oil		
Coolant		
Battery Water		
Battery Condition #1		
Battery Condition #2		
Transmission		
Engine Hours		
Fuel		
Water Tank		
Holding Tank		
Pumps/Bilge		
Seacocks		
Radio and Electronics		

Crew and Guests

Wind Force	Wind Direction	Sea State	Barometer	Forecast
0-5	N	Glassy	31.00	Fair
6-10	NE	Small Chop	30.75	Rising Wind
11-15	E	Moderate Chop	30.50	Veering Wind
16-20	SE	Heavy Chop	30.25	Backing Wind
21-25	S	Ground Swell	30.00	Squalls/Thunderstorms
26-30	SW	Crossing Seas	29.75	Rain
31-35	W	Boarding Seas	29.50	Fog
35-40	NW	Tide Rips	29.25	Storm
_____other	Variable		29.00	Haze

Time	Notes

Time			Pilotage	Course	Speed	Log	Miles	Comments from the Helm		
									Date:	
										Day:
									From:	
										To:
									Page	

Morning Checklist		
Check	Comment	Initial
Engine Oil		
Coolant		
Battery Water		
Battery Condition #1		
Battery Condition #2		
Transmission		
Engine Hours		
Fuel		
Water Tank		
Holding Tank		
Pumps/Bilge		
Seacocks		
Radio and Electronics		

Crew and Guests		

Wind Force	Wind Direction	Sea State	Barometer	Forecast
0-5	N	Glassy	31.00	Fair
6-10	NE	Small Chop	30.75	Rising Wind
11-15	E	Moderate Chop	30.50	Veering Wind
16-20	SE	Heavy Chop	30.25	Backing Wind
21-25	S	Ground Swell	30.00	Squalls/Thunderstorms
26-30	SW	Crossing Seas	29.75	Rain
31-35	W	Boarding Seas	29.50	Fog
35-40	NW	Tide Rips	29.25	Storm
_____other	Variable		29.00	Haze

Time	Notes

Time		Pilotage	Course	Speed	Log	Miles	Comments from the Helm
							Date: Day:
							From: To:
							Page

Morning Checklist		
Check	Comment	Initial
Engine Oil		
Coolant		
Battery Water		
Battery Condition #1		
Battery Condition #2		
Transmission		
Engine Hours		
Fuel		
Water Tank		
Holding Tank		
Pumps/Bilge		
Seacocks		
Radio and Electronics		

Crew and Guests

Wind Force	Wind Direction	Sea State	Barometer	Forecast
0-5	N	Glassy	31.00	Fair
6-10	NE	Small Chop	30.75	Rising Wind
11-15	E	Moderate Chop	30.50	Veering Wind
16-20	SE	Heavy Chop	30.25	Backing Wind
21-25	S	Ground Swell	30.00	Squalls/Thunderstorms
26-30	SW	Crossing Seas	29.75	Rain
31-35	W	Boarding Seas	29.50	Fog
35-40	NW	Tide Rips	29.25	Storm
_____other	Variable		29.00	Haze

Time	Notes

Time	Pilotage		Course	Speed	Log	Miles	Comments from the Helm
							Date:
							Day:
							From:
							To:
							Page

Morning Checklist		
Check	Comment	Initial
Engine Oil		
Coolant		
Battery Water		
Battery Condition #1		
Battery Condition #2		
Transmission		
Engine Hours		
Fuel		
Water Tank		
Holding Tank		
Pumps/Bilge		
Seacocks		
Radio and Electronics		
Radio and Electronics		
Radio and Electronics		

Crew and Guests		

Wind Force	Wind Direction	Sea State	Barometer	Forecast
0-5	N	Glassy	31.00	Fair
6-10	NE	Small Chop	30.75	Rising Wind
11-15	E	Moderate Chop	30.50	Veering Wind
16-20	SE	Heavy Chop	30.25	Backing Wind
21-25	S	Ground Swell	30.00	Squalls/Thunderstorms
26-30	SW	Crossing Seas	29.75	Rain
31-35	W	Boarding Seas	29.50	Fog
35-40	NW	Tide Rips	29.25	Storm
_____other	Variable		29.00	Haze

Time	Notes

Time	Pilotage	Course	Speed	Log	Miles	Comments from the Helm
						Date: Day:
						From: To:
						Page

Morning Checklist		
Check	Comment	Initial
Engine Oil		
Coolant		
Battery Water		
Battery Condition #1		
Battery Condition #2		
Transmission		
Engine Hours		
Fuel		
Water Tank		
Holding Tank		
Pumps/Bilge		
Seacocks		
Radio and Electronics		

Crew and Guests

Wind Force	Wind Direction	Sea State	Barometer	Forecast
0-5	N	Glassy	31.00	Fair
6-10	NE	Small Chop	30.75	Rising Wind
11-15	E	Moderate Chop	30.50	Veering Wind
16-20	SE	Heavy Chop	30.25	Backing Wind
21-25	S	Ground Swell	30.00	Squalls/Thunderstorms
26-30	SW	Crossing Seas	29.75	Rain
31-35	W	Boarding Seas	29.50	Fog
35-40	NW	Tide Rips	29.25	Storm
_____other	Variable		29.00	Haze

Time	Notes

Time		Pilotage	Course	Speed	Log	Miles	Comments from the Helm		
							Date:	Day:	
							From:	To:	
							Page		

Morning Checklist		
Check	Comment	Initial
Engine Oil		
Coolant		
Battery Water		
Battery Condition #1		
Battery Condition #2		
Transmission		
Engine Hours		
Fuel		
Water Tank		
Holding Tank		
Pumps/Bilge		
Seacocks		
Radio and Electronics		

Crew and Guests

Wind Force	Wind Direction	Sea State	Barometer	Forecast
0-5	N	Glassy	31.00	Fair
6-10	NE	Small Chop	30.75	Rising Wind
11-15	E	Moderate Chop	30.50	Veering Wind
16-20	SE	Heavy Chop	30.25	Backing Wind
21-25	S	Ground Swell	30.00	Squalls/Thunderstorms
26-30	SW	Crossing Seas	29.75	Rain
31-35	W	Boarding Seas	29.50	Fog
35-40	NW	Tide Rips	29.25	Storm
_____other	Variable		29.00	Haze

Time	Notes

Time	Pilotage	Course	Speed	Log	Miles	Comments from the Helm
						Date:
						Day:
						From:
						To:
						Page

Morning Checklist		
Check	Comment	Initial
Engine Oil		
Coolant		
Battery Water		
Battery Condition #1		
Battery Condition #2		
Transmission		
Engine Hours		
Fuel		
Water Tank		
Holding Tank		
Pumps/Bilge		
Seacocks		
Radio and Electronics		
Crew and Guests		

Wind Force	Wind Direction	Sea State	Barometer	Forecast
0-5	N	Glassy	31.00	Fair
6-10	NE	Small Chop	30.75	Rising Wind
11-15	E	Moderate Chop	30.50	Veering Wind
16-20	SE	Heavy Chop	30.25	Backing Wind
21-25	S	Ground Swell	30.00	Squalls/Thunderstorms
26-30	SW	Crossing Seas	29.75	Rain
31-35	W	Boarding Seas	29.50	Fog
35-40	NW	Tide Rips	29.25	Storm
_____other	Variable		29.00	Haze

Time	Notes

Time			Pilotage	Course	Speed	Log	Miles	Comments from the Helm		
									Day:	Date:
									To:	From:
									Page	

Morning Checklist		
Check	Comment	Initial
Engine Oil		
Coolant		
Battery Water		
Battery Condition #1		
Battery Condition #2		
Transmission		
Engine Hours		
Fuel		
Water Tank		
Holding Tank		
Pumps/Bilge		
Seacocks		
Radio and Electronics		

Crew and Guests

Wind Force	Wind Direction	Sea State	Barometer	Forecast
0-5	N	Glassy	31.00	Fair
6-10	NE	Small Chop	30.75	Rising Wind
11-15	E	Moderate Chop	30.50	Veering Wind
16-20	SE	Heavy Chop	30.25	Backing Wind
21-25	S	Ground Swell	30.00	Squalls/Thunderstorms
26-30	SW	Crossing Seas	29.75	Rain
31-35	W	Boarding Seas	29.50	Fog
35-40	NW	Tide Rips	29.25	Storm
_____other	Variable		29.00	Haze

Time	Notes

Time		Pilotage	Course	Speed	Log	Miles	Comments from the Helm
							Date: Day:
							From: To:
							Page

Morning Checklist

Check		Comment	Initial
Engine Oil			
Coolant			
Battery Water			
Battery Condition	#1		
	#2		
Transmission			
Engine Hours			
Fuel			
Water Tank			
Holding Tank			
Pumps/Bilge			
Seacocks			
Radio and Electronics			

Crew and Guests

Wind Force	Wind Direction	Sea State	Barometer	Forecast
0-5	N	Glassy	31.00	Fair
6-10	NE	Small Chop	30.75	Rising Wind
11-15	E	Moderate Chop	30.50	Veering Wind
16-20	SE	Heavy Chop	30.25	Backing Wind
21-25	S	Ground Swell	30.00	Squalls/Thunderstorms
26-30	SW	Crossing Seas	29.75	Rain
31-35	W	Boarding Seas	29.50	Fog
35-40	NW	Tide Rips	29.25	Storm
_____ other	Variable		29.00	Haze

Time	Notes

Time		Pilotage	Course	Speed	Log	Miles	Comments from the Helm
							Date: Day:
							From: To:
							Page

Morning Checklist		
Check	**Comment**	**Initial**
Engine Oil		
Coolant		
Battery Water		
Battery Condition #1		
Battery Condition #2		
Transmission		
Engine Hours		
Fuel		
Water Tank		
Holding Tank		
Pumps/Bilge		
Seacocks		
Radio and Electronics		

Crew and Guests

Wind Force	Wind Direction	Sea State	Barometer	Forecast
0-5	N	Glassy	31.00	Fair
6-10	NE	Small Chop	30.75	Rising Wind
11-15	E	Moderate Chop	30.50	Veering Wind
16-20	SE	Heavy Chop	30.25	Backing Wind
21-25	S	Ground Swell	30.00	Squalls/Thunderstorms
26-30	SW	Crossing Seas	29.75	Rain
31-35	W	Boarding Seas	29.50	Fog
35-40	NW	Tide Rips	29.25	Storm
_____other	Variable		29.00	Haze

Time	Notes

Time			Pilotage	Course	Speed	Log	Miles	Comments from the Helm		
										Date:
									Day:	
									To:	From:
									Page	

Morning Checklist		
Check	Comment	Initial
Engine Oil		
Coolant		
Battery Water		
Battery Condition #1		
Battery Condition #2		
Transmission		
Engine Hours		
Fuel		
Water Tank		
Holding Tank		
Pumps/Bilge		
Seacocks		
Radio and Electronics		

Crew and Guests

Wind Force	Wind Direction	Sea State	Barometer	Forecast
0-5	N	Glassy	31.00	Fair
6-10	NE	Small Chop	30.75	Rising Wind
11-15	E	Moderate Chop	30.50	Veering Wind
16-20	SE	Heavy Chop	30.25	Backing Wind
21-25	S	Ground Swell	30.00	Squalls/Thunderstorms
26-30	SW	Crossing Seas	29.75	Rain
31-35	W	Boarding Seas	29.50	Fog
35-40	NW	Tide Rips	29.25	Storm
_____other	Variable		29.00	Haze

Time	Notes

Time	Pilotage	Course	Speed	Log	Miles	Comments from the Helm
						Date: Day:
						From: To:
						Page

Morning Checklist		
Check	Comment	Initial
Engine Oil		
Coolant		
Battery Water		
Battery Condition #1		
Battery Condition #2		
Transmission		
Engine Hours		
Fuel		
Water Tank		
Holding Tank		
Pumps/Bilge		
Seacocks		
Radio and Electronics		

Crew and Guests

Wind Force	Wind Direction	Sea State	Barometer	Forecast
0-5	N	Glassy	31.00	Fair
6-10	NE	Small Chop	30.75	Rising Wind
11-15	E	Moderate Chop	30.50	Veering Wind
16-20	SE	Heavy Chop	30.25	Backing Wind
21-25	S	Ground Swell	30.00	Squalls/Thunderstorms
26-30	SW	Crossing Seas	29.75	Rain
31-35	W	Boarding Seas	29.50	Fog
35-40	NW	Tide Rips	29.25	Storm
_____other	Variable		29.00	Haze

Time	Notes

Time	Pilotage	Course	Speed	Log	Miles	Comments from the Helm
						Date:
						Day:
						From:
						To:
						Page

Morning Checklist		
Check	Comment	Initial
Engine Oil		
Coolant		
Battery Water		
Battery Condition #1		
Battery Condition #2		
Transmission		
Engine Hours		
Fuel		
Water Tank		
Holding Tank		
Pumps/Bilge		
Seacocks		
Radio and Electronics		

Crew and Guests

Wind Force	Wind Direction	Sea State	Barometer	Forecast
0-5	N	Glassy	31.00	Fair
6-10	NE	Small Chop	30.75	Rising Wind
11-15	E	Moderate Chop	30.50	Veering Wind
16-20	SE	Heavy Chop	30.25	Backing Wind
21-25	S	Ground Swell	30.00	Squalls/Thunderstorms
26-30	SW	Crossing Seas	29.75	Rain
31-35	W	Boarding Seas	29.50	Fog
35-40	NW	Tide Rips	29.25	Storm
_____other	Variable		29.00	Haze

Time	Notes

Time		Pilotage	Course	Speed	Log	Miles	Comments from the Helm	
							Day:	Date:
							To:	From:
							Page	

Morning Checklist		
Check	Comment	Initial
Engine Oil		
Coolant		
Battery Water		
Battery Condition	#1	
	#2	
Transmission		
Engine Hours		
Fuel		
Water Tank		
Holding Tank		
Pumps/Bilge		
Seacocks		
Radio and Electronics		

Crew and Guests

Wind Force	Wind Direction	Sea State	Barometer	Forecast
0-5	N	Glassy	31.00	Fair
6-10	NE	Small Chop	30.75	Rising Wind
11-15	E	Moderate Chop	30.50	Veering Wind
16-20	SE	Heavy Chop	30.25	Backing Wind
21-25	S	Ground Swell	30.00	Squalls/Thunderstorms
26-30	SW	Crossing Seas	29.75	Rain
31-35	W	Boarding Seas	29.50	Fog
35-40	NW	Tide Rips	29.25	Storm
_____ other	Variable		29.00	Haze

Time	Notes

Time		Pilotage	Course	Speed	Log	Miles	Comments from the Helm
							Date: Day:
							From: To:
							Page

Morning Checklist			
Check		Comment	Initial
Engine Oil			
Coolant			
Battery Water			
Battery Condition	#1		
	#2		
Transmission			
Engine Hours			
Fuel			
Water Tank			
Holding Tank			
Pumps/Bilge			
Seacocks			
Radio and Electronics			

Crew and Guests

Wind Force	Wind Direction	Sea State	Barometer	Forecast
0-5	N	Glassy	31.00	Fair
6-10	NE	Small Chop	30.75	Rising Wind
11-15	E	Moderate Chop	30.50	Veering Wind
16-20	SE	Heavy Chop	30.25	Backing Wind
21-25	S	Ground Swell	30.00	Squalls/Thunderstorms
26-30	SW	Crossing Seas	29.75	Rain
31-35	W	Boarding Seas	29.50	Fog
35-40	NW	Tide Rips	29.25	Storm
_____other	Variable		29.00	Haze

Time	Notes

Time	Pilotage		Course	Speed	Log	Miles	Comments from the Helm		
									Date:
								Day:	
									From:
								To:	
								Page	

Morning Checklist		
Check	Comment	Initial
Engine Oil		
Coolant		
Battery Water		
Battery Condition #1		
Battery Condition #2		
Transmission		
Engine Hours		
Fuel		
Water Tank		
Holding Tank		
Pumps/Bilge		
Seacocks		
Radio and Electronics		
Radio and Electronics		
Radio and Electronics		

Crew and Guests

Wind Force	Wind Direction	Sea State	Barometer	Forecast
0-5	N	Glassy	31.00	Fair
6-10	NE	Small Chop	30.75	Rising Wind
11-15	E	Moderate Chop	30.50	Veering Wind
16-20	SE	Heavy Chop	30.25	Backing Wind
21-25	S	Ground Swell	30.00	Squalls/Thunderstorms
26-30	SW	Crossing Seas	29.75	Rain
31-35	W	Boarding Seas	29.50	Fog
35-40	NW	Tide Rips	29.25	Storm
_____other	Variable		29.00	Haze

Time	Notes

Time	Pilotage	Course	Speed	Log	Miles	Comments from the Helm
						Date: Day:
						From: To:
						Page

Morning Checklist

Check		Comment	Initial
Engine Oil			
Coolant			
Battery Water			
Battery Condition	#1		
	#2		
Transmission			
Engine Hours			
Fuel			
Water Tank			
Holding Tank			
Pumps/Bilge			
Seacocks			
Radio and Electronics			

Crew and Guests

Wind Force	Wind Direction	Sea State	Barometer	Forecast
0-5	N	Glassy	31.00	Fair
6-10	NE	Small Chop	30.75	Rising Wind
11-15	E	Moderate Chop	30.50	Veering Wind
16-20	SE	Heavy Chop	30.25	Backing Wind
21-25	S	Ground Swell	30.00	Squalls/Thunderstorms
26-30	SW	Crossing Seas	29.75	Rain
31-35	W	Boarding Seas	29.50	Fog
35-40	NW	Tide Rips	29.25	Storm
_____ other	Variable		29.00	Haze

Time	Notes

Time	Pilotage	Course	Speed	Log	Miles	Comments from the Helm
						Date:
						Day:
						From:
						To:
						Page

Morning Checklist		
Check	Comment	Initial
Engine Oil		
Coolant		
Battery Water		
Battery Condition #1		
Battery Condition #2		
Transmission		
Engine Hours		
Fuel		
Water Tank		
Holding Tank		
Pumps/Bilge		
Seacocks		
Radio and Electronics		

Crew and Guests

Wind Force	Wind Direction	Sea State	Barometer	Forecast
0-5	N	Glassy	31.00	Fair
6-10	NE	Small Chop	30.75	Rising Wind
11-15	E	Moderate Chop	30.50	Veering Wind
16-20	SE	Heavy Chop	30.25	Backing Wind
21-25	S	Ground Swell	30.00	Squalls/Thunderstorms
26-30	SW	Crossing Seas	29.75	Rain
31-35	W	Boarding Seas	29.50	Fog
35-40	NW	Tide Rips	29.25	Storm
_____other	Variable		29.00	Haze

Time	Notes

Time	Pilotage	Course	Speed	Log	Miles	Comments from the Helm

Date:

Day:

From:

To:

Page

Morning Checklist		
Check	**Comment**	**Initial**
Engine Oil		
Coolant		
Battery Water		
Battery Condition #1		
Battery Condition #2		
Transmission		
Engine Hours		
Fuel		
Water Tank		
Holding Tank		
Pumps/Bilge		
Seacocks		
Radio and Electronics		

Crew and Guests

Wind Force	Wind Direction	Sea State	Barometer	Forecast
0-5	N	Glassy	31.00	Fair
6-10	NE	Small Chop	30.75	Rising Wind
11-15	E	Moderate Chop	30.50	Veering Wind
16-20	SE	Heavy Chop	30.25	Backing Wind
21-25	S	Ground Swell	30.00	Squalls/Thunderstorms
26-30	SW	Crossing Seas	29.75	Rain
31-35	W	Boarding Seas	29.50	Fog
35-40	NW	Tide Rips	29.25	Storm
_____other	Variable		29.00	Haze

Time	Notes

Time	Pilotage	Course	Speed	Log	Miles	Comments from the Helm
						Date: Day:
						From: To:
						Page

Morning Checklist

Check		Comment	Initial
Engine Oil			
Coolant			
Battery Water			
Battery Condition	#1		
	#2		
Transmission			
Engine Hours			
Fuel			
Water Tank			
Holding Tank			
Pumps/Bilge			
Seacocks			
Radio and Electronics			

Crew and Guests

Wind Force	Wind Direction	Sea State	Barometer	Forecast
0-5	N	Glassy	31.00	Fair
6-10	NE	Small Chop	30.75	Rising Wind
11-15	E	Moderate Chop	30.50	Veering Wind
16-20	SE	Heavy Chop	30.25	Backing Wind
21-25	S	Ground Swell	30.00	Squalls/Thunderstorms
26-30	SW	Crossing Seas	29.75	Rain
31-35	W	Boarding Seas	29.50	Fog
35-40	NW	Tide Rips	29.25	Storm
_____other	Variable		29.00	Haze

Time	Notes

Time		Pilotage	Course	Speed	Log	Miles	Comments from the Helm
							Date: Day:
							From: To:
							Page

Morning Checklist		
Check	Comment	Initial
Engine Oil		
Coolant		
Battery Water		
Battery Condition #1		
Battery Condition #2		
Transmission		
Engine Hours		
Fuel		
Water Tank		
Holding Tank		
Pumps/Bilge		
Seacocks		
Radio and Electronics		

Crew and Guests

Wind Force	Wind Direction	Sea State	Barometer	Forecast
0-5	N	Glassy	31.00	Fair
6-10	NE	Small Chop	30.75	Rising Wind
11-15	E	Moderate Chop	30.50	Veering Wind
16-20	SE	Heavy Chop	30.25	Backing Wind
21-25	S	Ground Swell	30.00	Squalls/Thunderstorms
26-30	SW	Crossing Seas	29.75	Rain
31-35	W	Boarding Seas	29.50	Fog
35-40	NW	Tide Rips	29.25	Storm
_____other	Variable		29.00	Haze

Time	Notes

Time	Pilotage	Course	Speed	Log	Miles	Comments from the Helm
						Date:
						Day:
						From:
						To:
						Page

Morning Checklist		
Check	Comment	Initial
Engine Oil		
Coolant		
Battery Water		
Battery Condition #1		
Battery Condition #2		
Transmission		
Engine Hours		
Fuel		
Water Tank		
Holding Tank		
Pumps/Bilge		
Seacocks		
Radio and Electronics		

Crew and Guests

Wind Force	Wind Direction	Sea State	Barometer	Forecast
0-5	N	Glassy	31.00	Fair
6-10	NE	Small Chop	30.75	Rising Wind
11-15	E	Moderate Chop	30.50	Veering Wind
16-20	SE	Heavy Chop	30.25	Backing Wind
21-25	S	Ground Swell	30.00	Squalls/Thunderstorms
26-30	SW	Crossing Seas	29.75	Rain
31-35	W	Boarding Seas	29.50	Fog
35-40	NW	Tide Rips	29.25	Storm
_____other	Variable		29.00	Haze

Time	Notes

Time	Pilotage	Course	Speed	Log	Miles	Comments from the Helm
						Date: Day:
						From: To:
						Page

Morning Checklist

Check		Comment	Initial
Engine Oil			
Coolant			
Battery Water			
Battery Condition	#1		
	#2		
Transmission			
Engine Hours			
Fuel			
Water Tank			
Holding Tank			
Pumps/Bilge			
Seacocks			
Radio and Electronics			

Crew and Guests

Wind Force	Wind Direction	Sea State	Barometer	Forecast
0-5	N	Glassy	31.00	Fair
6-10	NE	Small Chop	30.75	Rising Wind
11-15	E	Moderate Chop	30.50	Veering Wind
16-20	SE	Heavy Chop	30.25	Backing Wind
21-25	S	Ground Swell	30.00	Squalls/Thunderstorms
26-30	SW	Crossing Seas	29.75	Rain
31-35	W	Boarding Seas	29.50	Fog
35-40	NW	Tide Rips	29.25	Storm
_____other	Variable		29.00	Haze

Time	Notes

Time			Pilotage	Course	Speed	Log	Miles	Comments from the Helm
								Date:
								Day:
								From:
								To:
								Page

Morning Checklist			

Check		Comment	Initial
Engine Oil			
Coolant			
Battery Water			
Battery Condition	#1		
	#2		
Transmission			
Engine Hours			
Fuel			
Water Tank			
Holding Tank			
Pumps/Bilge			
Seacocks			
Radio and Electronics			

Crew and Guests

Wind Force	Wind Direction	Sea State	Barometer	Forecast
0-5	N	Glassy	31.00	Fair
6-10	NE	Small Chop	30.75	Rising Wind
11-15	E	Moderate Chop	30.50	Veering Wind
16-20	SE	Heavy Chop	30.25	Backing Wind
21-25	S	Ground Swell	30.00	Squalls/Thunderstorms
26-30	SW	Crossing Seas	29.75	Rain
31-35	W	Boarding Seas	29.50	Fog
35-40	NW	Tide Rips	29.25	Storm
_____other	Variable		29.00	Haze

Time	Notes

Time	Pilotage	Course	Speed	Log	Miles	Comments from the Helm
						Date: Day:
						From: To:
						Page

Morning Checklist		
Check	**Comment**	**Initial**
Engine Oil		
Coolant		
Battery Water		
Battery Condition #1		
Battery Condition #2		
Transmission		
Engine Hours		
Fuel		
Water Tank		
Holding Tank		
Pumps/Bilge		
Seacocks		
Radio and Electronics		

Crew and Guests

Wind Force	Wind Direction	Sea State	Barometer	Forecast
0-5	N	Glassy	31.00	Fair
6-10	NE	Small Chop	30.75	Rising Wind
11-15	E	Moderate Chop	30.50	Veering Wind
16-20	SE	Heavy Chop	30.25	Backing Wind
21-25	S	Ground Swell	30.00	Squalls/Thunderstorms
26-30	SW	Crossing Seas	29.75	Rain
31-35	W	Boarding Seas	29.50	Fog
35-40	NW	Tide Rips	29.25	Storm
_____other	Variable		29.00	Haze

Time	Notes

Time			Pilotage	Course	Speed	Log	Miles	Comments from the Helm		
									Date:
									Day:
									From:
									To:
									Page

Morning Checklist			
Check	**Comment**		**Initial**
Engine Oil			
Coolant			
Battery Water			
Battery Condition	#1		
	#2		
Transmission			
Engine Hours			
Fuel			
Water Tank			
Holding Tank			
Pumps/Bilge			
Seacocks			
Radio and Electronics			

Crew and Guests

Wind Force	Wind Direction	Sea State	Barometer	Forecast
0-5	N	Glassy	31.00	Fair
6-10	NE	Small Chop	30.75	Rising Wind
11-15	E	Moderate Chop	30.50	Veering Wind
16-20	SE	Heavy Chop	30.25	Backing Wind
21-25	S	Ground Swell	30.00	Squalls/Thunderstorms
26-30	SW	Crossing Seas	29.75	Rain
31-35	W	Boarding Seas	29.50	Fog
35-40	NW	Tide Rips	29.25	Storm
_____other	Variable		29.00	Haze

Time	Notes

Time		Pilotage	Course	Speed	Log	Miles	Comments from the Helm
							Date: Day:
							From: To:
							Page

Morning Checklist		
Check	Comment	Initial
Engine Oil		
Coolant		
Battery Water		
Battery Condition #1		
Battery Condition #2		
Transmission		
Engine Hours		
Fuel		
Water Tank		
Holding Tank		
Pumps/Bilge		
Seacocks		
Radio and Electronics		

Crew and Guests

Wind Force	Wind Direction	Sea State	Barometer	Forecast
0-5	N	Glassy	31.00	Fair
6-10	NE	Small Chop	30.75	Rising Wind
11-15	E	Moderate Chop	30.50	Veering Wind
16-20	SE	Heavy Chop	30.25	Backing Wind
21-25	S	Ground Swell	30.00	Squalls/Thunderstorms
26-30	SW	Crossing Seas	29.75	Rain
31-35	W	Boarding Seas	29.50	Fog
35-40	NW	Tide Rips	29.25	Storm
_____other	Variable		29.00	Haze

Time	Notes

Time		Pilotage	Course	Speed	Log	Miles	Comments from the Helm
							Date:
							Day:
							From:
							To:
							Page

Morning Checklist		
Check	Comment	Initial
Engine Oil		
Coolant		
Battery Water		
Battery Condition #1		
Battery Condition #2		
Transmission		
Engine Hours		
Fuel		
Water Tank		
Holding Tank		
Pumps/Bilge		
Seacocks		
Radio and Electronics		

Crew and Guests

Wind Force	Wind Direction	Sea State	Barometer	Forecast
0-5	N	Glassy	31.00	Fair
6-10	NE	Small Chop	30.75	Rising Wind
11-15	E	Moderate Chop	30.50	Veering Wind
16-20	SE	Heavy Chop	30.25	Backing Wind
21-25	S	Ground Swell	30.00	Squalls/Thunderstorms
26-30	SW	Crossing Seas	29.75	Rain
31-35	W	Boarding Seas	29.50	Fog
35-40	NW	Tide Rips	29.25	Storm
_____other	Variable		29.00	Haze

Time	Notes

Time		Pilotage	Course	Speed	Log	Miles	Comments from the Helm
							Date:
							Day:
							From:
							To:
							Page

Morning Checklist		
Check	Comment	Initial
Engine Oil		
Coolant		
Battery Water		
Battery Condition #1		
Battery Condition #2		
Transmission		
Engine Hours		
Fuel		
Water Tank		
Holding Tank		
Pumps/Bilge		
Seacocks		
Radio and Electronics		

Crew and Guests

Wind Force	Wind Direction	Sea State	Barometer	Forecast
0-5	N	Glassy	31.00	Fair
6-10	NE	Small Chop	30.75	Rising Wind
11-15	E	Moderate Chop	30.50	Veering Wind
16-20	SE	Heavy Chop	30.25	Backing Wind
21-25	S	Ground Swell	30.00	Squalls/Thunderstorms
26-30	SW	Crossing Seas	29.75	Rain
31-35	W	Boarding Seas	29.50	Fog
35-40	NW	Tide Rips	29.25	Storm
_____other	Variable		29.00	Haze

Time	Notes

Time		Pilotage	Course	Speed	Log	Miles	Comments from the Helm
							Date:
							Day:
							From:
							To:
							Page

Morning Checklist		
Check	Comment	Initial
Engine Oil		
Coolant		
Battery Water		
Battery Condition #1		
Battery Condition #2		
Transmission		
Engine Hours		
Fuel		
Water Tank		
Holding Tank		
Pumps/Bilge		
Seacocks		
Radio and Electronics		

Crew and Guests

Wind Force	Wind Direction	Sea State	Barometer	Forecast
0-5	N	Glassy	31.00	Fair
6-10	NE	Small Chop	30.75	Rising Wind
11-15	E	Moderate Chop	30.50	Veering Wind
16-20	SE	Heavy Chop	30.25	Backing Wind
21-25	S	Ground Swell	30.00	Squalls/Thunderstorms
26-30	SW	Crossing Seas	29.75	Rain
31-35	W	Boarding Seas	29.50	Fog
35-40	NW	Tide Rips	29.25	Storm
_____other	Variable		29.00	Haze

Time	Notes

Time		Pilotage	Course	Speed	Log	Miles	Comments from the Helm		
								Day:	Date:
								To:	From:
								Page	

Morning Checklist		
Check	Comment	Initial
Engine Oil		
Coolant		
Battery Water		
Battery Condition #1		
Battery Condition #2		
Transmission		
Engine Hours		
Fuel		
Water Tank		
Holding Tank		
Pumps/Bilge		
Seacocks		
Radio and Electronics		
Radio and Electronics		

Crew and Guests

Wind Force	Wind Direction	Sea State	Barometer	Forecast
0-5	N	Glassy	31.00	Fair
6-10	NE	Small Chop	30.75	Rising Wind
11-15	E	Moderate Chop	30.50	Veering Wind
16-20	SE	Heavy Chop	30.25	Backing Wind
21-25	S	Ground Swell	30.00	Squalls/Thunderstorms
26-30	SW	Crossing Seas	29.75	Rain
31-35	W	Boarding Seas	29.50	Fog
35-40	NW	Tide Rips	29.25	Storm
_____other	Variable		29.00	Haze

Time	Notes

Time		Pilotage	Course	Speed	Log	Miles	Comments from the Helm
							Date:
							Day:
							From:
							To:
							Page

Morning Checklist		
Check	Comment	Initial
Engine Oil		
Coolant		
Battery Water		
Battery Condition #1		
Battery Condition #2		
Transmission		
Engine Hours		
Fuel		
Water Tank		
Holding Tank		
Pumps/Bilge		
Seacocks		
Radio and Electronics		

Crew and Guests

Wind Force	Wind Direction	Sea State	Barometer	Forecast
0-5	N	Glassy	31.00	Fair
6-10	NE	Small Chop	30.75	Rising Wind
11-15	E	Moderate Chop	30.50	Veering Wind
16-20	SE	Heavy Chop	30.25	Backing Wind
21-25	S	Ground Swell	30.00	Squalls/Thunderstorms
26-30	SW	Crossing Seas	29.75	Rain
31-35	W	Boarding Seas	29.50	Fog
35-40	NW	Tide Rips	29.25	Storm
_____other	Variable		29.00	Haze

Time	Notes

Time			Pilotage	Course	Speed	Log	Miles	Comments from the Helm		
										Date:
									Day:	
										From:
									To:	
										Page

Morning Checklist		
Check	Comment	Initial
Engine Oil		
Coolant		
Battery Water		
Battery Condition #1		
Battery Condition #2		
Transmission		
Engine Hours		
Fuel		
Water Tank		
Holding Tank		
Pumps/Bilge		
Seacocks		
Radio and Electronics		

Crew and Guests

Wind Force	Wind Direction	Sea State	Barometer	Forecast
0-5	N	Glassy	31.00	Fair
6-10	NE	Small Chop	30.75	Rising Wind
11-15	E	Moderate Chop	30.50	Veering Wind
16-20	SE	Heavy Chop	30.25	Backing Wind
21-25	S	Ground Swell	30.00	Squalls/Thunderstorms
26-30	SW	Crossing Seas	29.75	Rain
31-35	W	Boarding Seas	29.50	Fog
35-40	NW	Tide Rips	29.25	Storm
_____other	Variable		29.00	Haze

Time	Notes

Time			Pilotage	Course	Speed	Log	Miles	Comments from the Helm		
										Date:
									Day:	
										From:
									To:	
									Page	

Morning Checklist

Check		Comment	Initial
Engine Oil			
Coolant			
Battery Water			
Battery Condition	#1		
	#2		
Transmission			
Engine Hours			
Fuel			
Water Tank			
Holding Tank			
Pumps/Bilge			
Seacocks			
Radio and Electronics			

Crew and Guests

Wind Force	Wind Direction	Sea State	Barometer	Forecast
0-5	N	Glassy	31.00	Fair
6-10	NE	Small Chop	30.75	Rising Wind
11-15	E	Moderate Chop	30.50	Veering Wind
16-20	SE	Heavy Chop	30.25	Backing Wind
21-25	S	Ground Swell	30.00	Squalls/Thunderstorms
26-30	SW	Crossing Seas	29.75	Rain
31-35	W	Boarding Seas	29.50	Fog
35-40	NW	Tide Rips	29.25	Storm
_____other	Variable		29.00	Haze

Time	Notes

Time	Pilotage	Course	Speed	Log	Miles	Comments from the Helm

Date:

Day:

From:

To:

Page

Morning Checklist		
Check	Comment	Initial
Engine Oil		
Coolant		
Battery Water		
Battery Condition #1		
Battery Condition #2		
Transmission		
Engine Hours		
Fuel		
Water Tank		
Holding Tank		
Pumps/Bilge		
Seacocks		
Radio and Electronics		

Crew and Guests

Wind Force	Wind Direction	Sea State	Barometer	Forecast
0-5	N	Glassy	31.00	Fair
6-10	NE	Small Chop	30.75	Rising Wind
11-15	E	Moderate Chop	30.50	Veering Wind
16-20	SE	Heavy Chop	30.25	Backing Wind
21-25	S	Ground Swell	30.00	Squalls/Thunderstorms
26-30	SW	Crossing Seas	29.75	Rain
31-35	W	Boarding Seas	29.50	Fog
35-40	NW	Tide Rips	29.25	Storm
_____other	Variable		29.00	Haze

Time	Notes

Time		Pilotage	Course	Speed	Log	Miles	Comments from the Helm
							Date:
							Day:
							From:
							To:
							Page

Morning Checklist		
Check	Comment	Initial
Engine Oil		
Coolant		
Battery Water		
Battery Condition #1		
Battery Condition #2		
Transmission		
Engine Hours		
Fuel		
Water Tank		
Holding Tank		
Pumps/Bilge		
Seacocks		
Radio and Electronics		

Crew and Guests

Wind Force	Wind Direction	Sea State	Barometer	Forecast
0-5	N	Glassy	31.00	Fair
6-10	NE	Small Chop	30.75	Rising Wind
11-15	E	Moderate Chop	30.50	Veering Wind
16-20	SE	Heavy Chop	30.25	Backing Wind
21-25	S	Ground Swell	30.00	Squalls/Thunderstorms
26-30	SW	Crossing Seas	29.75	Rain
31-35	W	Boarding Seas	29.50	Fog
35-40	NW	Tide Rips	29.25	Storm
_____other	Variable		29.00	Haze

Time	Notes

Time			Pilotage	Course	Speed	Log	Miles	Comments from the Helm		
									Day:	Date:
									To:	From:
									Page	

Morning Checklist		
Check	Comment	Initial
Engine Oil		
Coolant		
Battery Water		
Battery Condition #1		
Battery Condition #2		
Transmission		
Engine Hours		
Fuel		
Water Tank		
Holding Tank		
Pumps/Bilge		
Seacocks		
Radio and Electronics		

Crew and Guests

Wind Force	Wind Direction	Sea State	Barometer	Forecast
0-5	N	Glassy	31.00	Fair
6-10	NE	Small Chop	30.75	Rising Wind
11-15	E	Moderate Chop	30.50	Veering Wind
16-20	SE	Heavy Chop	30.25	Backing Wind
21-25	S	Ground Swell	30.00	Squalls/Thunderstorms
26-30	SW	Crossing Seas	29.75	Rain
31-35	W	Boarding Seas	29.50	Fog
35-40	NW	Tide Rips	29.25	Storm
_____other	Variable		29.00	Haze

Time	Notes

Time	Pilotage	Course	Speed	Log	Miles	Comments from the Helm
						Date:
						Day:
						From:
						To:
						Page

Morning Checklist

Check		Comment	Initial
Engine Oil			
Coolant			
Battery Water			
Battery Condition	#1		
	#2		
Transmission			
Engine Hours			
Fuel			
Water Tank			
Holding Tank			
Pumps/Bilge			
Seacocks			
Radio and Electronics			

Crew and Guests

Wind Force	Wind Direction	Sea State	Barometer	Forecast
0-5	N	Glassy	31.00	Fair
6-10	NE	Small Chop	30.75	Rising Wind
11-15	E	Moderate Chop	30.50	Veering Wind
16-20	SE	Heavy Chop	30.25	Backing Wind
21-25	S	Ground Swell	30.00	Squalls/Thunderstorms
26-30	SW	Crossing Seas	29.75	Rain
31-35	W	Boarding Seas	29.50	Fog
35-40	NW	Tide Rips	29.25	Storm
_____ other	Variable		29.00	Haze

Time	Notes

Time	Pilotage	Course	Speed	Log	Miles	Comments from the Helm
						Date: Day:
						From: To:
						Page

Morning Checklist		
Check	Comment	Initial
Engine Oil		
Coolant		
Battery Water		
Battery Condition #1		
Battery Condition #2		
Transmission		
Engine Hours		
Fuel		
Water Tank		
Holding Tank		
Pumps/Bilge		
Seacocks		
Radio and Electronics		

Crew and Guests		

Wind Force	Wind Direction	Sea State	Barometer	Forecast
0-5	N	Glassy	31.00	Fair
6-10	NE	Small Chop	30.75	Rising Wind
11-15	E	Moderate Chop	30.50	Veering Wind
16-20	SE	Heavy Chop	30.25	Backing Wind
21-25	S	Ground Swell	30.00	Squalls/Thunderstorms
26-30	SW	Crossing Seas	29.75	Rain
31-35	W	Boarding Seas	29.50	Fog
35-40	NW	Tide Rips	29.25	Storm
_____other	Variable		29.00	Haze

Time	Notes

Time	Pilotage	Course	Speed	Log	Miles	Comments from the Helm
							Date: Day:
							From: To:
							Page

Morning Checklist

Check		Comment	Initial
Engine Oil			
Coolant			
Battery Water			
Battery Condition	#1		
	#2		
Transmission			
Engine Hours			
Fuel			
Water Tank			
Holding Tank			
Pumps/Bilge			
Seacocks			
Radio and Electronics			

Crew and Guests

Wind Force	Wind Direction	Sea State	Barometer	Forecast
0-5	N	Glassy	31.00	Fair
6-10	NE	Small Chop	30.75	Rising Wind
11-15	E	Moderate Chop	30.50	Veering Wind
16-20	SE	Heavy Chop	30.25	Backing Wind
21-25	S	Ground Swell	30.00	Squalls/Thunderstorms
26-30	SW	Crossing Seas	29.75	Rain
31-35	W	Boarding Seas	29.50	Fog
35-40	NW	Tide Rips	29.25	Storm
_____other	Variable		29.00	Haze

Time	Notes

Time		Pilotage	Course	Speed	Log	Miles	Comments from the Helm		
								Day:	Date:
								To:	From:
								Page	

Morning Checklist		
Check	Comment	Initial
Engine Oil		
Coolant		
Battery Water		
Battery Condition #1		
Battery Condition #2		
Transmission		
Engine Hours		
Fuel		
Water Tank		
Holding Tank		
Pumps/Bilge		
Seacocks		
Radio and Electronics		

Crew and Guests

Wind Force	Wind Direction	Sea State	Barometer	Forecast
0-5	N	Glassy	31.00	Fair
6-10	NE	Small Chop	30.75	Rising Wind
11-15	E	Moderate Chop	30.50	Veering Wind
16-20	SE	Heavy Chop	30.25	Backing Wind
21-25	S	Ground Swell	30.00	Squalls/Thunderstorms
26-30	SW	Crossing Seas	29.75	Rain
31-35	W	Boarding Seas	29.50	Fog
35-40	NW	Tide Rips	29.25	Storm
_____other	Variable		29.00	Haze

Time	Notes

Time	Pilotage	Course	Speed	Log	Miles	Comments from the Helm		
								Date:
							Day:	
								From:
							To:	
							Page	

Morning Checklist		
Check	Comment	Initial
Engine Oil		
Coolant		
Battery Water		
Battery Condition #1		
Battery Condition #2		
Transmission		
Engine Hours		
Fuel		
Water Tank		
Holding Tank		
Pumps/Bilge		
Seacocks		
Radio and Electronics		
Radio and Electronics		

Crew and Guests

Wind Force	Wind Direction	Sea State	Barometer	Forecast
0-5	N	Glassy	31.00	Fair
6-10	NE	Small Chop	30.75	Rising Wind
11-15	E	Moderate Chop	30.50	Veering Wind
16-20	SE	Heavy Chop	30.25	Backing Wind
21-25	S	Ground Swell	30.00	Squalls/Thunderstorms
26-30	SW	Crossing Seas	29.75	Rain
31-35	W	Boarding Seas	29.50	Fog
35-40	NW	Tide Rips	29.25	Storm
_____other	Variable		29.00	Haze

Time	Notes

Time	Pilotage		Course	Speed	Log	Miles	Comments from the Helm		
									Date:
								Day:	
								To:	From:
								Page	

Morning Checklist

Check		Comment	Initial
Engine Oil			
Coolant			
Battery Water			
Battery Condition	#1		
	#2		
Transmission			
Engine Hours			
Fuel			
Water Tank			
Holding Tank			
Pumps/Bilge			
Seacocks			
Radio and Electronics			

Crew and Guests

Wind Force	Wind Direction	Sea State	Barometer	Forecast
0-5	N	Glassy	31.00	Fair
6-10	NE	Small Chop	30.75	Rising Wind
11-15	E	Moderate Chop	30.50	Veering Wind
16-20	SE	Heavy Chop	30.25	Backing Wind
21-25	S	Ground Swell	30.00	Squalls/Thunderstorms
26-30	SW	Crossing Seas	29.75	Rain
31-35	W	Boarding Seas	29.50	Fog
35-40	NW	Tide Rips	29.25	Storm
_____other	Variable		29.00	Haze

Time	Notes

Time		Pilotage	Course	Speed	Log	Miles	Comments from the Helm
							Date:
							Day:
							From:
							To:
							Page

Morning Checklist		
Check	Comment	Initial
Engine Oil		
Coolant		
Battery Water		
Battery Condition #1		
Battery Condition #2		
Transmission		
Engine Hours		
Fuel		
Water Tank		
Holding Tank		
Pumps/Bilge		
Seacocks		
Radio and Electronics		

Crew and Guests

Wind Force	Wind Direction	Sea State	Barometer	Forecast
0-5	N	Glassy	31.00	Fair
6-10	NE	Small Chop	30.75	Rising Wind
11-15	E	Moderate Chop	30.50	Veering Wind
16-20	SE	Heavy Chop	30.25	Backing Wind
21-25	S	Ground Swell	30.00	Squalls/Thunderstorms
26-30	SW	Crossing Seas	29.75	Rain
31-35	W	Boarding Seas	29.50	Fog
35-40	NW	Tide Rips	29.25	Storm
_____ other	Variable		29.00	Haze

Time	Notes

Time	Pilotage	Course	Speed	Log	Miles	Comments from the Helm
						Date: Day:
						From: To:
						Page

Morning Checklist		
Check	Comment	Initial
Engine Oil		
Coolant		
Battery Water		
Battery Condition #1		
Battery Condition #2		
Transmission		
Engine Hours		
Fuel		
Water Tank		
Holding Tank		
Pumps/Bilge		
Seacocks		
Radio and Electronics		
Radio and Electronics		
Radio and Electronics		

Crew and Guests

Wind Force	Wind Direction	Sea State	Barometer	Forecast
0-5	N	Glassy	31.00	Fair
6-10	NE	Small Chop	30.75	Rising Wind
11-15	E	Moderate Chop	30.50	Veering Wind
16-20	SE	Heavy Chop	30.25	Backing Wind
21-25	S	Ground Swell	30.00	Squalls/Thunderstorms
26-30	SW	Crossing Seas	29.75	Rain
31-35	W	Boarding Seas	29.50	Fog
35-40	NW	Tide Rips	29.25	Storm
_____other	Variable		29.00	Haze

Time	Notes

Time		Pilotage	Course	Speed	Log	Miles	Comments from the Helm		
									Date:
								Day:	
								To:	From:
								Page	

Morning Checklist		
Check	Comment	Initial
Engine Oil		
Coolant		
Battery Water		
Battery Condition #1		
Battery Condition #2		
Transmission		
Engine Hours		
Fuel		
Water Tank		
Holding Tank		
Pumps/Bilge		
Seacocks		
Radio and Electronics		

Crew and Guests

Wind Force	Wind Direction	Sea State	Barometer	Forecast
0-5	N	Glassy	31.00	Fair
6-10	NE	Small Chop	30.75	Rising Wind
11-15	E	Moderate Chop	30.50	Veering Wind
16-20	SE	Heavy Chop	30.25	Backing Wind
21-25	S	Ground Swell	30.00	Squalls/Thunderstorms
26-30	SW	Crossing Seas	29.75	Rain
31-35	W	Boarding Seas	29.50	Fog
35-40	NW	Tide Rips	29.25	Storm
_____other	Variable		29.00	Haze

Time	Notes

Time	Pilotage		Course	Speed	Log	Miles	Comments from the Helm		
								Day:	Date:
								To:	From:
								Page	

TO REORDER

The International
Marine

LOG BOOK

Please contact:

The McGraw-Hill Companies
Customer Service Department
P.O. Box 547
Blacklick, OH   43004
Retail Customers: 1-800-262-4729
Bookstores: 1-800-722-4726